Author
Ebru GUNGELEN

Proofread by
Astrid KLEINEGRIS

Interior Design
Yazardan Direct Team

Cover Design
Cosmo Publishing

Publisher
Cosmo Publishing Company
Austin, Texas
USA

Audio Scripts Read by
Mario Enrique VARGAS, Ru HAN

ISBN: 978-1-949872-17-0

©All rights reserved, including the rights of reproduction in whole or in part of any form. No parts of this book may be reproduced or transmitted in any form or by any means, electronic or mechanical, including photocopying, recording or by any information storage and retrieval system, without written permission from the author, except for the inclusions of brief quotations in a review.

TOEFL Junior TEST BOOK

(Journey to TOEFL IBT)

3 Practice Tests (with reviews and test-taking strategies)

This book is designed for students who desire to get high scores at the
TOEFL tests

EBRU GUNGELEN

Contents

ABOUT THE AUTHOR 7

Section 1

INTRODUCTION

- About the TOEFL JUNIOR Test (Scopes and Mapping of TOEFL Junior Standard scores to the CEFR) 11

- Quick review of each part of the test
  (Important tips on how to answer each skill part in the test) 13

Section 2

PRACTICE TEST

Practice Test-1

- Listening Comprehension 21
- Language Form and Meaning 30
- Reading Comprehension 39

Practice Test-2

- Listening Comprehension 55
- Language Form and Meaning 63
- Reading Comprehension 69

Practice Test-3

- Listening Comprehension 85
- Language Form and Meaning 94
- Reading Comprehension 102

Section 3

LISTENING SCRIPTS

- Practice Test 1 117
- Practice Test 2 125
- Practice Test 3 132

Section 4

ANSWER KEYS

- Practice Test 1 141
- Practice Test 2 142
- Practice Test 3 143

About The Author

Ebru Gungelen was born in Antalya, TURKEY (1971). She graduated from Dokuz Eylul University, Foreign Languages Department, Faculty of Education, as an English teacher. She has been a professional teacher of English for 30 years. She has experience of teaching all age groups, from primary students to adults. During her teaching career, she worked as a Vice Principal of a secondary school, and before that worked as the head of the English department at a private school. She worked as an English teacher in both secondary and high schools. Before she got retired, she worked at Mediterranean University and ran the language courses at AKUNSEM (Mediterranean University Lifelong Education Center).

Since then she has been preparing students to both national and international exams (Cambridge Exams(KET-PET-FCE) , IELTS-TOEFL). She is also working as an education consultant to those who would like to study abroad, **CELT Education Abroad-www.celttour.com (cg@celttour.com)**

Courses and certificates:

- British Council-Certificate in English Language Teaching for Young Learners
- British Council-Teacher Training Course (How to become a teacher trainer)
- British Council- Agent and Counsellor Training
- Sidmouth International School, UK- Preparing students to UCLAS exams and how to write tests for FCE-KET-PET-CAE-CPE (she took courses from the exam makers of Cambridge University in England with a group of ELT teachers from other continents)
- Many other educational courses

Her previously published books are;
GRAMMARPACE (Series of four books including TestBooks (CEFR A1-A2-B1)) – published by KEY Publishing, 2016
Summer books for young children, 2015
Her ongoing projects are;
How to write an academic essay
ELT Skills book (CEFR A1-A2-B1)
Academic Dictionary for TOEFL exams

A Word From The Author

The tests in this book will provide a standard and consistent measure of your proficiency level of English, which is recognized worldwide. This test book meets the ETS standards and is based upon international assessments of English language proficiency for both young, K-12 students and young adult learners. The tests and the tips given in this book will help you prepare yourselves for the TOEFL IBT. As the TOEFL tests are universally recognised, this book will appeal to all ESL learners around the world.

To sum up, the test is not appropriate for those who have not yet attained a basic level of proficiency.
I hope my book will be of great help and all of you will take the advantage of my questions during your journey to the TOEFL tests.

Wish you all the best and success.

Ebru GUNGELEN

Section 1
INTRODUCTION

ABOUT THE TEST

INTRODUCTION
IN GENERAL THE TOEFL JUNIOR STANDARD TEST;

- is a practical tool to measure EFL learners' progress in English-language skills
- serves as a placement test
- helps learners develop their English language communication skills for their future studies related to English
- prepares EFL, or ESL learners to TOEFL IBT, TOEFL PBT, TOEFL ITP tests.

THE STRUCTURE OF THE TEST

- It is a paper-based test
- It consists of 126 multiple-choice questions
- It includes three sections; each contains 42 questions:
  1-) **Listening Comprehension:** It measures the listening ability of the students to understand English for academic purposes
  2-) **Language Form and Meaning:** It measures the ability and the capability of the students to do the exercises that test skills such as grammar and vocabulary in context
  3-) **Reading Comprehension:** It meaures the reading ability of the students to understand both academic and non-academic texts (letters, notes, messages, announcements, etc.)
- The total testing time is **1 hour 55 minutes**

Sections	Number Of Questions	Time
Listening Comprehension	42	40 minutes
Language Form and Meaning	42	25 minutes
Reading Comprehension	42	50 minutes
TOTAL	126	1 hour 55 minutes

THE PROCEDURES OF THE TEST

- The test is given one session on the date and at the time and location arranged by an official of the institution that is administrating the test.
- Left-handed test-takers are advised to inform the test administrators before their seating is arranged.
- Test-takers are provided with a clock in the testing room and a blank note-taking paper for the Listening section.
- Test takers are allowed to bring along their black-lead pencils with erasers.

The following items are not allowed;

- Any kind of bags, backpacks, etc.
- Books, dictionaries, digitals, etc.
- Calculators, watches, etc.
- Cell phones, tablets, Ipads, etc.

- Food or beverages (unless approved due to a health related need)
- Hats, or headwear (unless by religious requirement)
- Mechanical or highlighted pens, pencils, any kind of disturbing appliances
- Listening devices
- Papers of any kind
- Copying, scanning or photographic devices

IMPORTANT WARNING: If a test-taker needs to take a break during the test, the answer sheet will be held by the test administrator and extra time will not be given to the student. All the test takers are expected to obey the rules, if not their tests will not be assessed and no scores will be reported for them.

THE SCORE STRUCTURE OF THE TEST

- TOEFL Junior Standard test scores are determined by the number of questions that are answered correctly. The number of correct answers on each section is converted to a scale that ranges from 200 to 300 that is presented in the table below

Sections	Score Range
Listening Comprehension	200-300
Language Form and Meaning	200-300
Reading Comprehension	200-300
Total Scrore	600-900

- In order to determine the students' proficiency level according to the CEFR Level (Common European Framework of Reference), the following table shows how the equivalances of the overall scores.

Overall Score Level	Total Scale Score	Certificated Color	Cefr Equivalance
5 Superior	845-900	Gold	B2 for all sections
4 Accomplished	785-840	Silver	B1 for all sections
3 Expanding	730-780	Bronze	Mostly B1 for all sections, but occassionally A2
2 Progressing	655-725	Green	Mostly A2 for all sections, but occassionally A1 for Reading and Listening
1 Emerging	600-650	Blue	Mostly A1 for Listening and Reading; mostly A2 for Language Form and Meaning

- The students' scores on sections are mapped to the Common European Framework of Reference to help them see what their scores mean on a global scale; as shown below:

Sections of the test	Below A2	CEFR level A2	CEFR level B1	CEFR level B2
Listening Comprehension	Under 225	225-245	250-285	290-300
Language Form and Meaning	Under 210	210-245	250-275	280-300
Reading Comprehension	Under 210	210-240	245-275	280-300

- ***IMPORTANT WARNING:*** Each section of the test has a fixed time limit. During the test, the test administrators tell the test-takers when to start and finish each part, so even if the test taker completes a section earlier than others, he/she may not go on to the next section. If they do so, they will be considered cheating and their scores will be cancelled.

QUICK REVIEW OF EACH PART OF THE TEST

LISTENING COMPREHENSION SECTION

The aim of this section is to test students' ability to listen and comprehend academic and non-academic talks.

There are ***three types*** of listening questions;

1st type: This part contains 10 short talks with one question for each talk. The talks are made by a principal, teacher, or other school staff member talking to students.

2nd type: This part contains interpersonal short conversations followed by three or four questions.

3rd type: This part contains talks or discussions about academic topics. Each talk or discussion is followed by three, four or five questions. This part tests the students' comprehension ability to understand academic texts.

TIPS ON HOW TO DO THE LISTENING SECTION

- Try to take good notes on the blank paper you have been given. While taking notes, focus on the key words that can give you an idea about the content of the question. **Dates, numbers, names, locations, items, any excuse or reasons** given for an action are the most important key points that should be written down as you listen.
- Do not write in full letters while taking notes during the listening. Try to invent your creative note-taking symbols, abbreviations, etc; for example write **"st"** instead of **"student"**.

- In order not to be confused by who said what while listening to two speakers, it is advisable to make a small table by dividing it into two sections and showing the similar points with "=" and the adverse ideas by putting an "X", as shown below:

1st speaker (male) –you can use a symbol for "male" as "ml"	2nd speaker (female)- you can use a symbol for female as "fm"
√ join the cmp. (means he agrees to join the competition-you may create your own symbols to save time while taking note)	= (just putting this symbol will make it easier for you to remember that the female speaker agrees with the male speaker- or you may create your own symbol-but just try to save time because conversations move fast during the listening section.) X (if you use this cross symbol, it will remind you that the female speaker doesn't agree with the male speaker.)

Try to invent your own symbols and abbreviations, then practise this by listening to various audio materials.

- Introductory information given before the listening starts is another key element that you should focus on. For instance; the narrator may say; "Now listen to a conversation between a science teacher and a student" In this case; you must get the idea that the subject of the conversation will be related to anything about science; it can be about the student's science project or an invention in science, or something connected with the subject matter.
- In short; listen to who the speakers are by identifying their professions, their relationships, and so on.
- Try to focus on the intonations of the speakers while they are talking, in this way you may find it easy to understand their feelings and emotions. If the speaker uses some specific words while putting a lot of stress on them, it is apparent that the speaker may be annoyed, worried or frustrated. This will give you the gist of the main idea of the conversation.
- While listening to academic texts, focus on the names, dates, locations, living conditions and so on. For instance; the listening can be about animals in danger. Take crucial notes on the reasons and what precautions are taken or should be taken. Once you hear what you are going to listen about, try to imagine what could be said about that and then focus on the key words that will help you take in mind while taking notes.

LANGUAGE AND FORM SECTION

The aim of this section is to test students' ability to demonstrate proficiency in key language skills of English and to evaluate how much they know about the grammatical structures and vocabulary of English language. It mainly tests the vocabulary and grammar in context.

This section contains emails, letters, announcements, short fictional passages, magazine articles and passages from textbooks.

TIPS ON HOW TO DO THE LANGUAGE AND FORM SECTION

- There are some basic points that you should put your attention on. For example; punctuation marks are key points that will help you while choosing the correct word or phrase in the question box:

For example: Seagulls
(A) that
(B) which
(C) ,that
(D) ,which

are related to the Family of Sternidae, learn, remember and pass on behaviors.

The correct answer to the question is **"D"**, because the information given in between two commas "," show that it is extra information which doesn't define the subject, so a non-defining relative pronoun should be used here. "That" cannot be used as a non-defining relative pronoun after a comma ",".

Here, we see that if you hesitate while choosing the best alternative, just pay attention to the punctuation marks and consider whether there should be a colon, semi comma or a full stop before or after the word given before or after the question box.

- Capital letters are also very important to identify the correct answer. In some cases, there can be two possible correct answers in the box, but the capital letters may help you choose the correct answer:

For example: I'd love to meet you on Sunday.
(A) However,
(B) but
(C) so
(D) Because

I will be busy studying for my finals.

Here, we see that "however" and "but" are two possible answers, but the first sentence is completed with a full stop(.) in the end. This shows that the word following the second sentence will have to start with a capital letter. So the answer to this question is **"A"**.

- Singular and plural nouns will help you find the correct answer. You should be careful with count and noncount words. *For example;* if the sentence starts with a singular noun, it should be followed with a singular verb.

For example: The information which
| (A) have been |
| (B) is |
| (C) are |
| (D) has |
given by the authority is incorrect.

The noun "information" is a singular uncountable word, so it should be followed by a singular verb. In this question the correct answer is **"B"**, because it is a singular verb and this is a passive sentence. Even though the alternative **"D"** has a singular verb, the sentence with that would be an active sentence, because the main verb after the question box shows that we have a passive statement.

- Pay attention to the tense agreement in the sentences. If the sentence starts with a present time, it cannot be followed by a past perfect tense if there is not a past time given

For example; He said all the things that
| (A) happen |
| (B) is happening |
| (C) had happened |
| (D) has happened |
before he retired were unforgettable.

Here, we see that the narrator is talking about a past event, so the correct answer to this question is **"C"**. The two sentences are related to each other.

- In short, there must be an agreement in all cases; between nouns and verbs, between pronouns and related subjects. In order to answer correctly, you should pay attention more and try to focus on the correct grammar and correct vocabulary item to choose.

READING COMPREHENSION SECTION

The aim of this section is to test students' ability to read and comprehend academic and non-academic texts. There are several types of reading texts in this section;

1st type: Short texts; announcements made by a school authority, teacher or an expert, announcements or informative articles

2nd type: E-mails, letters, notes

3rd type: Academic texts

TIPS ON HOW TO DO THE READING SECTION

- Underline the key words; focus on the nouns, dates, locations, reasons, contradictions, numbers.

- Read the question and underline the key word in the question and then skim the passage to find the matching information or the parallel idea given by the question.
- The idea given in the question may be a restatement of the idea given in the text.

For example; The teachers in the board have **reached a compromise** with the school administrators to apply the new exam system.

Imagine that this sentence appeared in the passage and the question is as follows;

What is the <u>outcome</u> of the meeting between teachers and the school administrators about the new exam system?

(A) They haven't come to the same point.
(B) They have come to an agreement.
(C) There have opposing ideas.
(D) They have decided to apply a new exam system.

The correct answer to this question is **"B"**, because "reached a compromise" is the restatement of "come to an agreement".

- To identify the main idea of the passage of a paragraph, you should skim the text carefully by identifying the key words. Then focus on what is repeatedly mentioned in the texts, do not focus on the details and examples much.
- Do not forget that main ideas are mostly given in the first lines of a text. The statements given after the main topic are the supporting ideas; such as examples, verifications, etc.
- Each paragraph tells us about different topics related to the main subject of the text. So, it will be easy for you to take brief notes next to each paragraph to remind you about what was mentioned in that paragraph.

    For example; when a question related to a third paragraph appears, you will find it easy to locate in which paragraph you should look for the answer to that question. It will help you save your time. Do not attempt to reread every line in the paragraphs.

    For example; Imagine that a paragraph starts with a sentence like this:

    There are <u>two main factors</u> that affect human race to resist _____

    First, underline the words, then note which factors are mentioned in that paragraph. So, it will help you find the correct answer to the question that is related to it.

In short, focus on the main idea, key words, time order (events given in an order), sequencing events. Try to paraphrase the statements, find the matching words or phrases.

Section 2

PRACTICE TEST

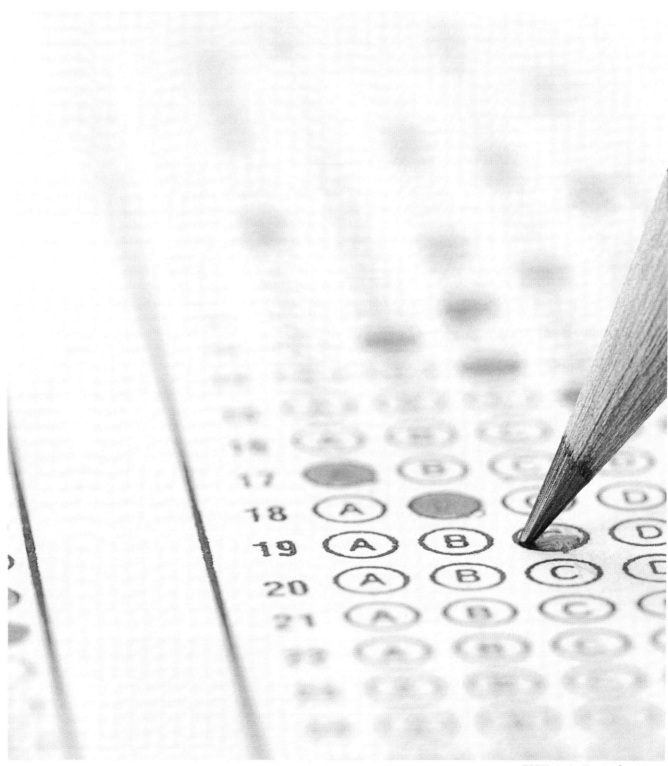

Test 1

Paper 1: Listening Comprehension
Time: 40 Minutes
42 Questions

The listening section has 42 questions. Follow along as you listen to the directions to the listening section.

DIRECTIONS

In this section of the test, you will hear conversations, announcements or instructions. Each conversation, announcement or instruction is followed by one question. Choose the best answer to each question and mark the letter of the correct answer on your answer sheet. You will hear each conversation, announcement or instruction only one time. You will have enough time to transfer your answers from the question paper to the answer sheet at the end of the listening section.

Here is an example:

What does the woman mean?

(A) She will attend the meeting soon.
(B) She will have to miss the meeting.
(C) She thinks she will not be invited to the meeting.
(D) She has to be somewhere else at the time of the meeting.

The correct answer is (B), "She will have to miss the meeting."

Here is another example:

What are the speakers talking about?

(A) Their summer time activities
(B) Going on a vacation
(C) Spring festival
(D) An upcoming test

The correct answer is (C), "Spring festival".

Go on to the next page, and the test will begin with question number one.

Audio recordings of this section can be accessed by scanning this QR code on your device

You will hear ten (10) short conversations. Each conversation is followed by one question. Choose the best answer to each question and mark the letter of the correct answer on your answer sheet. You will hear the listening ONCE.

Part 1

Listen to a high school principal making an announcement.

Answer question 1
1) Which one is not true according to the announcement?

(A) The program will be held in the first week of April.
(B) The participant students must fill in a registration form.
(C) The students will be given breakfast and packed lunch.
(D) Students will use their own way of transportation.

Listen to a high school principal talking to the students.

Answer question 2
2) What is the main subject of the announcement?

(A) State when the exact date of the elections will be
(B) Inform students about the upcoming elections to choose student leaders
(C) Let students learn about the members of the school board
(D) Ask all the students to write down their names on the candidate list

Listen to a language teacher making an announcement at the end of the lesson.

Answer question 3
3) Why does the teacher want the students to do the progress check questions?

(A) to revise the subjects they have completed so far
(B) to cover all the units they have done up to now
(C) to complete the exercises in the workbook
(D) to start a new unit

Listen to a scientist making a speech to high school students.

Answer question 4
4) How will the scientist most probably finish this sentence?

(A) the technology used at universities.
(B) how humans make use of the improving technology.
(C) how people are addicted to VR.
(D) the negative effects of VR.

Listen to a principal making an announcement to students.

Answer question 5
5) Which one is not true according to the announcement?

(A) The new counsellor is going to arrange private programs with individual students.
(B) The new counsellor is going to monitor students' success.
(C) Mr. Bringley is the retired counsellor.
(D) Mrs. Watson got retired on age grounds.

Listen to a principal making an announcement to parents.

Answer question 6
6) What is this announcement mainly for?

(A) to help children move on to the next level of their studies
(B) to invite parents to attend school workshops
(C) to give some advice to parents
(D) to encourage students to study harder

Part 1

Listen to what a science teacher says about extinction.

Answer question 7
7) Which one is not a natural cause of extinction according to the speech?

(A) Cosmic radiation
(B) Human causes of extinction
(C) Severe weather conditions
(D) Changing sea levels

Listen to a doctor making a speech.

Answer question 8
8) The symptoms that the doctor mentions indicate that one may _____.

(A) have indigestion problems
(B) feel dizziness and weakness
(C) have coronary artery disease
(D) suffer from heartburn

Listen to an expert talking about deforestation.

Answer question 9
9) Urbanization, meaning using land for housing _____.

(A) is one of the biggest reasons for destroying forests.
(B) causes people to lose their homelands.
(C) causes the Earth to lose over 20 million acres of forests.
(D) results in climate change.

Listen to an education consultant making a speech to students.

Answer question 10
10) What is the main topic of the talk?

(A) How to avoid negative thoughts
(B) How to gain effective studying habits
(C) Learning about your own skills
(D) The distractions that affect students' concentration

You will hear a conversation between a student and a teacher. It is followed by five questions. Choose the best answer to each question and mark the letter of the correct answer on your answer sheet. You will hear the listening ONCE.

Part 2

Listen to a boy talking to his teacher, Mrs. Wellsh and answer questions 11 to 15.

Answer question 11
11) Why does the boy want to speak to his teacher?

(A) to talk about his sports scholarship
(B) to get an extension on his assignment
(C) to ask for help with his studies
(D) to talk about the topic of his essay

Answer question 12
12) What is the topic of the essay?

(A) technological innovations
(B) sports scholarships
(C) basketball tournaments
(D) career development

Answer question 13
13) What does the teacher really mean when she says; "You must get your priorities straight."?

(A) that he has to be more focused on his scholarship
(B) that he should consider what he should do for his career
(C) that he needs to study harder and be more attentive
(D) that he must focus on his attention and concern on which is most important to him

Answer question 14
14) Which one is <u>not true</u> according to the conversation?

(A) Brian must attend all the matches, because he can't risk his scholarship.
(B) Brian plays basketball in the college team.
(C) Brian wants to achieve a scholarship.
(D) Brian has a sports scholarship.

Answer question 15
15) How does the conversation end?

(A) The teacher doesn't reject Brian's request.
(B) Brian gives in and apologizes.
(C) Brian asks for a two-week extension.
(D) The teacher accepts to give Brian an extension, but not for now.

You will hear a conversation between two friends. It is followed by six questions. Choose the best answer to each question and mark the letter of the correct answer on your answer sheet. You will hear the listening ONCE.

Part 3

Listen to a boy talking to his friend and answer questions 16 to 21.

Answer question 16
16) What are the speakers mainly talking about?

(A) The match James played the other day
(B) Steward's future career plans
(C) The team's next games
(D) James's desire to play in the school team

Answer question 17
17) Jane congratulates James on
_____.

(A) doing double major at school
(B) his new project
(C) winning the match
(D) his success at school

Answer question 18
18) What can be inferred about James's performance?

(A) He made quite a lot of saves.
(B) He played so well that he scored three goals.
(C) He is an outstanding goalkeeper.
(D) He is the best player in the team.

Answer question 19
19) What does Jane mean by exclaiming "How come!" after James talks about his lesson load at school?

(A) to show her excitement
(B) to show her surprise
(C) to show her dislike
(D) to show her enthusiasm

Answer question 20
20) Why is James doing a double major?

(A) to support his father financially
(B) to start working as soon as he graduates
(C) to be occupied with more work load
(D) to have more options and opportunities in his future career

Answer question 21
21) What can be inferred about education costs according to James's words?

(A) affordable
(B) very cheap
(C) very expensive
(D) not a problem

You will hear a conversation between a father and a girl. It is followed by five questions. Choose the best answer to each question and mark the letter of the correct answer on your answer sheet. You will hear the listening ONCE.

Part 4

Listen to a girl talking to her father and answer questions 22 to 26.

Answer question 22
22) What is the mood of the father?

(A) happy
(B) excited
(C) furious
(D) cheerful

Answer question 23
23) Why is the room so messy?

(A) The girl is writing a story, so she doesn't have time to clean the room.
(B) The girl threw torn paper sheets all around the room.
(C) The father is tidying his daughter's room.
(D) The room hasn't been cleaned up for days.

Answer question 24
24) What is the father complaining about?

(A) The due date is very soon.
(B) His daughter has joined a contest without his permission.
(C) His daughter's spending too much time on the net.
(D) The girl hasn't completed her writing yet.

Answer question 25
25) What does the father mean by saying "If only you would spend more time on reading books than wasting your time on the net"?

(A) He is complaining about his daughter's spending too much time on the internet.
(B) He is contented with his daughter's spending time efficiently.
(C) He thinks his daughter spends more time reading than using the net.
(D) He feels regretful that he has given a laptop to his daughter.

Answer question 26
26) In the end, what does the father suggest her?

(A) concentrate on the cash prize
(B) tidy up the room then start her work
(C) rest for a while then start writing
(D) turn off the laptop and not use the mobile phone

You will hear a biologist talking about how bees communicate. It is followed by four questions. Choose the best answer to each question and mark the letter of the correct answer on your answer sheet. You will hear the listening ONCE.

Part 5

Listen to a biologist talking about how bees communicate and then answer questions 27 to 30.

Answer question 27
27) What information does the talk start with?

(A) how bees communicate
(B) how bees use senses to find the flowers to make honey
(C) what bees do while looking for the best flower
(D) what worker bees are called

Answer question 28
28) How do worker bees tell the others where the best flowers are?

(A) They suck the nectar from the flower.
(B) They use color, smell, shape, location and time of day.
(C) They use a special language to tell the others.
(D) They store the nectar in their special honey stomach.

Answer question 29
29) What is the word "waggle" used for?

(A) how bees dance
(B) worker bees
(C) scout bees
(D) the colony

Answer question 30
30) According to the talk, which is not true?

(A) Worker bees are called honey bee workers.
(B) Worker bees communicate by dancing.
(C) Dancing extremely fast means there is a lot of food.
(D) If the worker bees find food nearby, they do not dance.

You will hear a historian talking about two ancient civilizations. It is followed by six questions. Choose the best answer to each question and mark the letter of the correct answer on your answer sheet. You will hear the listening ONCE.

Part 6

Listen to a historian talking about two ancient civilizations and then answer questions 31 to 36.

Answer question 31
31) What is the main idea of the talk?

(A) The pharaohs were Egyptian kings.
(B) Epyptians had great values.
(C) There are differences between two ancient civilizations.
(D) Egyptians practised religion.

Answer question 32
32) What does the historian imply about ziggurats?

(A) They are less known than the pyramids.
(B) Their constructions took years to finish.
(C) They were built in Egypt.
(D) They look bigger than the pyramids.

Answer question 33
33) What is the similarity between a pyramid and a ziggurat?

(A) Pyramids were built in Egypt, but ziggurats were built in Mesopotamia.
(B) They are both large structures.
(C) Their sizes are different.
(D) The Egyptian pyramid is more triangular.

Answer question 34
34) How is a ziggurat different from a pyramid?

(A) It has steps on the sides.
(B) It is made of different type of material.
(C) It has various types.
(D) It is older than a pyramid.

Answer question 35
35) Why are there stairs on the sides of a ziggurat?

(A) to keep the tombs of the priests in the temple.
(B) to pray to Mesopotamian Gods
(C) to reach the temple at the top
(D) to give a different style

Answer question 36
36) Why does the historian talk about the pharaohs?

(A) To talk about their importance in the society
(B) To note that they had the pyramids to be their tombs
(C) To show their role in their society
(D) To talk about their value

You will hear part of a speech given in a Social Studies class. It is followed by six questions. Choose the best answer to each question and mark the letter of the correct answer on your answer sheet. You will hear the listening ONCE.

Part 7

Listen to a teacher talking and then answer questions 37 to 42.

Answer question 37
37) What is the teacher mainly talking about?

(A) Towns in West Virginia
(B) How the Green Bank Telescope works
(C) The world's most precise telescope
(D) Black holes and comets

Answer question 38
38) What makes this telescope so special?

(A) It has been used by scientists for decades.
(B) It was built by NRAO.
(C) It is one-of-a kind because of its accurateness.
(D) It is located in a small town.

Answer question 39
39) Which of the following is not true according to the lesson?

(A) Scientists have been using this telescope to search for comets, stars and black holes.
(B) Scientists to use this telescope must be American.
(C) Education programs are also provided by NRAO.
(D) Over 1000 scientists have used the telescope in the last 10 years.

Answer question 40
40) Why is the area where the telescope is located called "Quiet Zone"?

(A) The residents in that area never socialize with each other, so they live in their own quiet world.
(B) Because devices that connect to the internet are banned.
(C) Because the residents prefer to live quietly.
(D) It is an uninhabited area.

Answer question 41
41) We can infer from the talk that "Wireless telecommunication devices _____."

(A) are used on inside the construction in which the telescope is located.
(B) are obligatory in and around the town of Green Bank.
(C) are used only in the Quiet Zone.
(D) are forbidden to prevent any kind of signal from interfering with the telescope's work.

Answer question 42
42) What is a surveillance truck used for?

(A) It works for the national radio to check the traffic.
(B) It detects the area to find criminals that violate other residents' rights.
(C) It patrols the town to check radio frequencies.
(D) It is used to prevent people from coming into the town.

Test 1

Paper 2: Language Form And Meaning
Time: 25 Minutes
42 Questions

The Language Form and Meaning section has 42 questions. Follow along as you read the directions to the Language Form and Meaning Section.

DIRECTIONS

In this section of the test, you will finish the sentences by picking the correct word or words. The boxes contain the answers that are available to choose from. Choose the best answer to each question and mark the letter of the correct answer on your answer sheet.

Here are two sample questions:

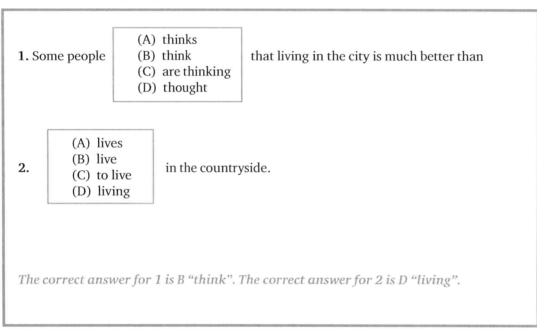

1. Some people
   (A) thinks
   (B) think
   (C) are thinking
   (D) thought
   that living in the city is much better than

2.
   (A) lives
   (B) live
   (C) to live
   (D) living
   in the countryside.

The correct answer for 1 is B "think". The correct answer for 2 is D "living".

Part 1

Questions 1 - 4 refer to the following email.

Hello, Lisa!

I am really sorry that you haven't been able to come to school. It's been a week now. I hope

1. you
   - (A) are getting
   - (B) have felt
   - (C) cannot get
   - (D) may feel

better, because I am scared that you will have

2. trouble in coping with the lessons. Now I
   - (A) will write
   - (B) wrote
   - (C) am writing
   - (D) haven't written

to let you know

3. about the topics of the upcoming exams. You know our final exams
   - (A) will have started
   - (B) were supposed to start
   - (C) have started
   - (D) start

next week. I hope you will come this Friday. Then we can study and review the lessons

4. together.
   - (A) Not hesitate to call
   - (B) Don't hesitate to call
   - (C) Hesitate not calling
   - (D) Hesitated to call

me. You can send a message by email if you need any help for

your questions. I'll always help you, you know that.

PS. I've attached the list of the exam topics.

Part 2

Questions 5 - 8 refer to the following email.

Hi, Andrew!

5. Thanks for
(A) to call
(B) calling
(C) called
(D) call
me. It was great to hear

6.
(A) from
(B) to
(C) in
(D) at
you, because I was having a horrible day. I

7.
(A) work
(B) was working
(C) worked
(D) works
on a project when you called. I couldn't talk much.

8. Sorry for that. I felt so tense at that time, because I was
(A) with
(B) on
(C) in
(D) at
the beginning of my work and I was

not feeling so sure whether I could finish it on time or not. Fortunately, I was able to complete and hand it in on time. It was a great relief in the end.

How are you? I hope everything's fine.

Shall we meet up on the weekend? I'll call you later.

Bye.

Mike.

Part 3

Questions 9 - 12 refer to the following email.

Dear Aunt Katie,

9. Thank you so much for the wonderful present. That was very kind
   (A) of
   (B) for
   (C) at
   (D) with

10. you. I am sure this microwave
    (A) did
    (B) has
    (C) will be
    (D) wash
    very useful here,

because there is only one in the school dormitory and there's one kitchen for

11. ten student rooms. This
    (A) makes hard to
    (B) is hard to make
    (C) makes it hard
    (D) made hard
    to use the microwave there, so I'll keep this one in

my room. It's very handy.

Well, I am enjoying my life here. I'm interested in sociology, and I think I am really good at it.

12. I hope
    (A) to see
    (B) for seeing
    (C) saw
    (D) see
    you during summer vacation when the schools close.

I've gotta go now.

Kisses to everyone at home.

Love,

Alison.

Part 4

Questions 13 - 16 refer to the following email.

Hello, Sue!

13. I am sorry for
(A) didn't call
(B) to call not
(C) not calling
(D) not have called
you back yesterday. I was in Mr. Jacobs's

14. room when you rang. He is our school principal. So I had to
(A) hang up
(B) answer
(C) respond
(D) call back
.

You can imagine how stressful I was at that time. I was called in to the

15. principal's room by the student affairs officer while we were
(A) having
(B) doing
(C) making
(D) getting
an experiment in the

science lab. You know what it means if you are called by the principal!

16. However, I was sure I hadn't done anything wrong.
(A) Beside
(B) After
(C) Just as
(D) Because
I was entering the principal's

room, his secretary said that it wasn't me that he wanted to see. It was another girl who had the same name as mine. You can't imagine how relieved I was!

Anyway, I'll call you tomorrow.

Bye, take care.

Jane XXX

Part 5

Questions 17 - 20 refer to the following email.

Hi Joe!

Thanks for your email. I'd be very happy to go out with you some time. You told me that

17. you'd like to see me
    (A) during
    (B) inside
    (C) while
    (D) between
    the week, but I have to say that I

18. am kind of busy. I am staying after school and
    (A) studied
    (B) will be studying
    (C) have studied
    (D) was studying
    in the school library with

a friend who is really good at biology this week, because this Friday we are going to take the final exam, and I am really bad at it. He is helping me to revise the subjects. So every day this week I will be busy studying. If it's

19. okay, can we meet up next weekend instead? I'm really looking
    (A) at
    (B) into
    (C) up
    (D) forward
    to

20. seeing you. I've got
    (A) much
    (B) a lot
    (C) many
    (D) a little
    of things to tell you.

Take care.

Bye.

Lucinda.

Part 6

Questions 21 - 26 refer to the following magazine article.

21. Forests play a critical role in climate change, because they _____
(A) absorb
(B) absorbs
(C) absorbed
(D) have absorbed

22. carbon dioxide and other gases. These are the gases _____
(A) during
(B) where
(C) that
(D) why

23. contribute a lot to the greenhouse effect. _____ , these gases would be free in the
(A) Otherwise
(B) Because
(C) Just
(D) That's why

atmosphere, which is very dangerous for all living things.

24. Forests have another important role. _____ than three hundred million people live in forests and
(A) A lot
(B) More
(C) Much
(D) As

they depend on forests for their livestocks, which means they supply their food from forests. Forests provide habitat for plants and animals. They protect our watersheds and they also supply the oxygen, which is

25. necessary for us _____ . The most biologically diverse and complex forests are tropical
(A) surviving.
(B) to survive.
(C) survival.
(D) survivor.

rainforests. Temperatures are always warm there, and rainfall is abundant. However, forests are being destroyed. In the end, 15% of all greenhouse gas emissions are the result of this.

26. We must _____ urgent steps to do something against deforestation.
(A) to take
(B) took
(C) take
(D) to be taken

Part 7

Questions 27 - 34 refer to the following email.

27. The first ancient Olympic Games
- (A) that are known to held
- (B) that is known to hold
- (C) knows to hold
- (D) known to be held

were around 780 BC.

28. The games played in those years
- (A) that are dedicated
- (B) were dedicated
- (C) dedicate
- (D) is dedicating

to the Olympian gods.

29. They were held in the city
- (A) calls
- (B) was called
- (C) calling
- (D) called

Olympia. That's why, these games are still called "Olympic Games".

30. The ancient Olympic games lasted
- (A) for
- (B) at
- (C) in
- (D) from

over 12 centuries. The first

31. modern version of the Olympic games
- (A) were hold
- (B) were held
- (C) holding
- (D) was held

in the city of Athens,

32. 33.
- (A) the
- (B) which the
- (C) of the
- (D) of which

capital of Greece. These games

- (A) taking part
- (B) was taken part
- (C) took part
- (D) were taken part

34. in 1896. The idea
- (A) presenting
- (B) was presented
- (C) presents
- (D) presented

by a Frenchman, named Baron Pierre de Coubertin.

Part 8

Questions 35 - 42 refer to the following magazine article.

35. Healthy eating
- (A) is not
- (B) does not
- (C) doesn't mean
- (D) has not

about following strict diets. You don't

36. 37. need
- (A) being
- (B) be
- (C) to be
- (D) to have been

extremely thin.
- (A) Instead
- (B) Furthermore,
- (C) Almost
- (D) Therefore,

38. you don't have to deprive yourself
- (A) on
- (B) from
- (C) for
- (D) of

the delicious meals you love.

39. 40. You ought
- (A) replace
- (B) to replace
- (C) replacing
- (D) not replace

processed food that you constantly eat
- (A) with
- (B) from
- (C) at
- (D) by

41. real, natural, homemade food whenever possible. Every human being
- (A) need
- (B) was needed
- (C) needs
- (D) needed

a balance of protein, carbohydrates, fiber, vitamins and minerals in their diets. These help

42. them to
- (A) sustain
- (B) supress
- (C) stay
- (D) provide

a healthy mind and body.

Test 1

Paper 3: Reading Comprehension
Time: 50 Minutes
42 Questions

DIRECTIONS

In this part of the test, you will read **five (5)** articles and then read a total of **forty-two (42)** questions. After reading the questions, pick the appropriate answer and then mark that letter on the answer sheet.

Here is a sample article.

Sample Text

> Have you ever ridden a tuk tuk? Do you know what tuk tuk is? A tuk tuk is a three-wheeled vehicle that is used as a taxi in Bangkok. This vehicle is a kind of rickshaw that has a small engine fitted in. It is ideal for short-distant trips. As it is a very small vehicle, you don't get stuck in heavy traffic in Bangkok's busy roads. It is both convenient and cheap for commuters.

Example question 1.
1. What is this text mainly about?

(A) Means of transportation
(B) Why people prefer a tuk tuk
(C) What a tuk tuk is
(D) How to travel around Bangkok

The correct answer is *C, "What a tuk tuk is"*.

Example question 2.
2. Which one is wrong according to the text?

(A) Tuk tuks are ideal for short trips.
(B) Tuk tuks are convenient and cheap.
(C) Tuk tuks are three-wheeled.
(D) Tuk tuks are like cars with four wheels.

The correct answer is *D, "Tuk tuks are like cars with four wheels"*.

Part 1

Read the following announcement that a school principal makes and answer questions 1 - 7.

Attention to all, please! This year all the clubs will be done after school on Fridays. We have **reduced** the lesson hours from 7 to 5 so that you will have more free time and that you can join the clubs. As you will see, there are four categories. You are supposed to choose one of **them**. We'll give you a form in which you will write your name under the club name you have chosen. I hope you'll enjoy the clubs and take part in good projects. For further questions, ask Mrs. Andrews, our Vice Principal.

Categories	Name of the clubs	Objectives	What to expect
Subject Area Club	Art, Drama, Science, Math, Literature, History and Language	To improve interest and knowledge in a subject area taught in class.	Visit museums, art galleries, theaters and science and technology exhibits.
Hobby Club	Chess, Board and Video Games	To have a good time with your friends	Take part in chess and board game tournaments.
Sports Club	Outdoor and Indoor sports	To get socialized in groups, and be physically active	Visit sports centers, meet famous sports people
Charity Club	Fund raising for children/ animals/ homeless people	To create awareness and help others in need.	Visit wildlife rescue centers, help collecting money for people in need

1) What is the main purpose of the announcement?

(A) To inform the students about the clubs and what they include
(B) To let students learn about where to apply for the clubs
(C) To have students' further questions
(D) To introduce the new Vice Principal to students

2) In line 2, the word "reduced" is closest in meaning to _____.

(A) raised
(B) improved
(C) increased
(D) lessened

Part 1

3) What does "them" refer to in line 4?

(A) Subject area clubs
(B) The categories
(C) The hours of lessons
(D) Name of the students

4) What does the principal suggest that students do if they have further questions?

(A) Ask him during the announcement
(B) Join the clubs
(C) Ask them to the vice principal
(D) Put their names on the list

5) Which category is best for students who are interested in museums?

(A) Subject area club
(B) Hobby club
(C) Sports club
(D) Charity club

6) All categories include visits to some places, EXCEPT FOR _____ .

(A) Subject area club
(B) Hobby club
(C) Sports club
(D) Charity club

(7) According to the table, which one is the main objective of the charity club?

(A) Be physically active
(B) Create awareness
(C) Have a good time with friends
(D) Improve knowledge in subject areas

Read the following email and answer questions 8 - 12.

New Message

To	: Mark
From	: Frank
Subject:	Cancellation

1   Hi Mark,

My mom said you called today, then I tried to reach you. However, you didn't respond. I thought you could be in class then decided to write this email. I was going to call you anyway, because I have to let you know that our final match has been canceled. The other day our coach had a meeting with us, saying that he was **supposed** to travel to Los Angeles, where he would have to attend the "National Sports Seminar". He said that he would be back two weeks later. I couldn't get in touch then. I didn't know where you were. Were you ill? You weren't around at school.

9   I haven't seen you today, either. What's up? Are you in some kind of trouble?
Please let me know.

We should meet and talk. I'll try to reach you on the phone again.

Call me.
Frank

Send

---

8) What is the main reason of Frank writing this email to Mark?

(A) To let him know that their coach will travel to Los Angeles
(B) To invite him out for dinner
(C) To say that the final match has been canceled
(D) To ask him for a favor

9) What other phrase can we use instead of "supposed" in line 5?

(A) admitted
(B) expected
(C) hoped
(D) accepted

Part 2

10) According to the email, why has the final match been canceled?

(A) The players will attend a seminar
(B) The players won't be in town
(C) There will be heavy rain
(D) The coach will be away

11) Frank says he hasn't seen Mark around. How might he feel about it?

(A) worried
(B) happy
(C) excited
(D) accepted

12) What will Frank probably do next?

(A) go to the seminar
(B) call Mark on the phone
(C) visit Mark's home
(D) cancel the match

Part 3

Read the story and answer questions 13 - 19.

The School Dance

1   This is my first year in this school. So far I have made very few friends but they are not my besties. It's hard to get used to a new school system and new friends. I remember the day when my dad came home and told us that we were moving to Los Angeles. He was so excited about his new job, but he
5   didn't see my disappointment.

      How many times do we have to move? We had already changed five cities until we came to LA!
That was really enough. Each time we moved, I was having problems making friends and getting accustomed to a new school!

10   Anyway! Here I am. I am like an **alien** again! It is really embarrassing to start school in the middle of the school year! Nobody cared about me in the beginning until one day a girl came near me and said;
"Hi, I am Sue. I'd like to be your friend. Can I sit next to you?"
"Oh, sure. My name is Maria. Please take a seat." I said happily.

15   That was the start of a good friendship. Then she introduced me to her friends, She is not a popular girl at school, but she is calm and polite. I should say that she is very friendly, too. In general, I am trying to cope with everything new here! I'm surviving!

      Last Saturday night, I went to my first school dance party. You know what!
20   It was a **DISASTER!** If only I had thought about what I was going to wear a bit more sensibly. When I asked Sue, she said; "Just wear something that makes you feel comfortable ." Then I thought everybody would dress up for the night and that I shouldn't be so casual and then I wore a long dress which made me look so grown-up with high- heeled shoes. When I got there, some girls started
25   giggling. Everybody was in jeans and T-shirts. How could I be so stupid! Then I saw Sue coming. She said; "What's up? Why do you look so upset?"

      "Sue, why didn't you tell me to wear something casual?"; I asked.
"Come on, darling. You look great. Don't care about others, they are laughing, because they are jealous. You are the only girl that looks the most beautiful in
30   this hall.", she said. "Let's dance and have fun! ", she pulled me to the dance floor. We danced all night long. Not to mention the disastrous start, I can say that the rest of the night was worth everything! Because Sue made me feel like a princess!
To me, "Friendship is the most precious jewelery."

Part 3

13) Maria is upset about moving to a new city. Which of the following is not one of her reasons?

(A) She finds it hard to make friends.
(B) She doesn't feel safe in a new city.
(C) It's not easy to cope with a new life.
(D) It takes time to get used to a new school system.

14) How many cities have Maria and her parents seen so far?

(A) 6
(B) 5
(C) 1
(D) 2

15) In line 20, the word "alien" is closest in meaning to _____.

(A) a familiar thing
(B) a new student
(C) a creature out of this world
(D) something new

16) The word "disaster" in line 14 means _____.

(A) something great
(B) an unfortunate event
(C) an unforgettable moment
(D) an unbelievable experience

17) According to the story, during the first days of the new school, nobody spoke to Maria EXCEPT for _____.

(A) Sue
(B) the teachers
(C) her father
(D) other girls

18) Maria probably felt _____ when girls laughed at her at the dance party.

(A) excited
(B) embarrassed
(C) interested
(D) proud

19) What does Maria point out by saying; "Friendship is the most precious jewelry."

(A) importance and value of friendship
(B) how precious jewelery is
(C) value of jewelry
(D) importance of jewelery

Part 4

Read the magazine article and answer questions 20 - 26.

1   A mixed-breed dog, called Laika was the first living being in an orbit that was sent to space. She was launched on the Soviet Union's Sputnik 2, in 1957. It was stunning to witness this historical experiment at that time, because technology was not that much improved then as it is today.

5   Laika was not the only animal to **orbit** Earth. Astronauts have studied all kinds of animals – like wasps, ants, bees, frogs, mice, rats, snails, cockroaches, monkeys, even jellyfish since **then**. Laika was a Siberian husky. She was rescued from the streets of Moscow. Soviet Scientists thought that a stray dog would endure **harsh** conditions better than others, because this dog had

10   already lived under difficult conditions.

Laika was trained for space, fed by nutritious gels that would be her food in space. Unfortunately, the result of this experiment was a failure. Sputnik 2 burned up in the upper atmosphere in April, 1958.

It is still not known exactly how long Laika lived in orbit and what really

15   happened that caused the Sputnik got burnt.

The aim of these experiments are all for human beings. Is it possible for us to live in space? Can we survive?

20) Which title best summarizes the article?

(A) Laika, the first animal in space
(B) Astronauts in space
(C) New experiments
(D) Harsh conditions in space

21) In line 5, the word "orbit" is closest in meaning to _____ .

(A) transmit
(B) send
(C) launch
(D) move around

22) According to the text, all the following statements are true EXCEPT FOR _____ .

(A) Laika was a mix-breed dog.
(B) It was launched on an American spacecraft.
(C) Laika was rescued from the streets of Moscow.
(D) Laika was not the only animal that was sent to space.

Part 4

23) *Why did the astronauts think that this dog would be the best to endure the conditions in space?*

(A) This dog had already lived under hard conditions on the streets.
(B) Dogs are suitable for hard conditions.
(C) Laika was fed by nutritious gels, which made him strong.
(D) Other animals were also sent to space, but it wasn't a success.

24) *In line 7, what does "then" refer to ?*

(A) astronauts sent other animals to space
(B) 1958
(C) the time when Sputnik 2 was launched with Laika
(D) 20th century

25) *In line 8, the word "harsh" is closest in meaning to* _____

(A) specific
(B) difficult
(C) easy
(D) unusual

26) *The result of this experiment was* _____

(A) a failure
(B) a success
(C) stunning
(D) amazing

Part 5

Read the text and answer questions 27 - 36.

1   Almost 70% of the Australian mainland is covered with arid deserts. As a result, this makes Australia the driest inhabited continent on Earth, which means only 3% of the Australian population live in these areas. There are ten deserts; the Great Victoria Desert, Great Sandy Desert, Tanami Desert,
5   Simpson Desert, Gibson Desert, Little Sandy Desert, Strzelecki Desert, Sturt Stony Desert, Tirari Desert, Pedirka Desert. The main reason for the formation of these deserts is their location. Deserts are found in areas with less than 250 mm/yr of rainfall. They have long periods of drought, with little or no rain. They receive their **infrequent** rain in a short period of time.
10
   As a summary; any rainfall or flood water that deserts receive is rapidly evaporated if it is not soaked into the soil the moment it falls. Interestingly, another characteristic of deserts is that especially in winter, the night time temperature can drop to freezing, even after an extremely hot day. All deserts have a climate of extremes, from drought-flood to hot-freezing.

15   The desert climate also known as an arid climate, is a climate in which precipitation is too low to sustain any vegetation at all, which means rain, snow, hail that falls to doesn't stay in the soil well enough to help any vegetation grow.

27) What is the first paragraph mainly about?

(A) arid deserts in Australia
(B) formation of the deserts in Australia
(C) amount of rainfall in deserts
(D) vegetation in deserts

28) According to the text, the following statements are true EXCEPT FOR_____

(A) Deserts are arid areas.
(B) There are ten deserts in Australia.
(C) 70% of Australia mainland is inhabited.
(D) There is very little rainfall in deserts

29) We can infer from the text that _____

(A) deserts are areas where there is too much vegetation.
(B) there is a short period of drought in deserts.
(C) 3% of Australian population prefer living in areas where there is enough rainfall.
(D) location plays an important role in formation of deserts.

Part 5

30) In line 8, what does "infrequent" mean?

(A) rare
(B) often
(C) much
(D) almost

31) According to the text, what can be said about Australia?

(A) Australia is the driest inhabited continent.
(B) It is the most populated continent.
(C) Drought cannot be seen in Australian deserts due to sufficient rainfall.
(D) Deserts in Australia are always cold.

32) "Any rainfall or flood water that deserts receive is rapidly evaporated." With this statement, we can conclude that _____

(A) Australian deserts have enough rainfall and flood water.
(B) Rainfall or flood water evaporizes very quickly in deserts.
(C) Drought is the main problem in deserts.
(D) There is less water that evaporates than it sustains.

33) In line 10, we can use _____ instead of "As a summary".

(A) However
(B) Afterwards
(C) To sum up
(D) In consequence of

34) What is the weather like at night times in deserts?

(A) really hot
(B) freezing cold
(C) damp
(D) dry but hot

35) Why is the climate extreme in deserts?

(A) Because it has a variety of changes from drought-flood to hot-freezing.
(B) Because the weather is predictable.
(C) Because it has harsh weather conditions.
(D) Because the weather is always stable, not changeable.

36) What is "desert climate" also known as?

(A) extreme
(B) arid climate
(C) sustain
(D) infrequent

Part 6

Read the text and answer questions 37 - 42.

1   When we talk about the effects of climate changes around the World, the first thing that would come to our minds will be the environmental consequences; like rising sea levels, changes in the temperature or melting glaciers.

5   There are also bigger **consequences**; In other words, the results that occur because of climate change; one of which is flooding (mainly caused by rising of sea levels and melting of icebergs). In order to take precautions against flooding, wastewater treatment plants are being designed with flood gates. The other one, which is the biggest problem that our universe has been

10 facing for so long is Global Warming. **That** affects everything on Earth. Due to Global Warming, drought has become the major problem. For instance; every year water levels in dams are getting lower and lower because of insufficient rain.

Moreover, climate change is shaking up everything from finance to health.

15 Every nation should take important steps to avoid climate-related disasters like drought, hurricanes, flood, melting of icebergs, earthquakes, and all others. Because it is difficult to know exactly how dramatic the effects of climate change will be, it is hard to know how much it will affect various industries, too.

37) What is the text mainly about?

(A) Global Warming
(B) effects of climate change
(C) amount of rainfall
(D) precautions

38) According to the text, the following statements are true EXCEPT FOR _____

(A) Drought has become the major problem caused by Global Warming.
(B) Rising sea levels and melting of icebergs cause flooding.
(C) There are environmental consequences of climate change.
(D) Global Warming is the least important problem

Part 6

39) In line 4, what does "consequences" probably mean?

(A) changes
(B) affects
(C) reasons
(D) results

40) In line 10, what does the pronoun "that" refer to?

(A) Melting of icebergs
(B) Rising of sea levels
(C) Water level in dams
(D) Global Warming

41) Why are wastewater treatment plants designed with flood gates?

(A) to take precautions against flooding.
(B) to cause sea level rise
(C) to avoid drought
(D) to lessen the effects of Global Warming.

42) What is the main reason of the loss of water in dams?

(A) too much rain
(B) melting of icebergs
(C) insufficient rainfall
(D) efficient precautions

Section 2

PRACTICE TEST 2

Test 2

Paper 1: Listening Comprehension
Time: 40 Minutes
42 Questions

The listening section has 42 questions. Follow along as you listen to the directions to the listening section.

DIRECTIONS

In this section of the test, you will hear conversations, announcements or instructions. Each conversation, announcement or instruction is followed by one question. Choose the best answer to each question and mark the letter of the correct answer on your answer sheet. You will hear each conversation, announcement or instruction only one time. You will have enough time to transfer your answers from the question paper to the answer sheet at the end of the listening section.

Here is an example:

What does the woman mean?

(E) She will attend the meeting soon.
(F) She will have to miss the meeting.
(G) She thinks she will not be invited to the meeting.
(H) She has to be somewhere else at the time of the meeting.

The correct answer is (B), "She will have to miss the meeting."

Here is another example:

What are the speakers talking about?

(E) Their summer time activites
(F) Going on a vacation
(G) Spring festival
(H) An upcoming test

The correct answer is (C), "Spring festival".

Go on to the next page, and the test will begin with question number one.

Audio recordings of this section can be accessed by scanning this QR code on your device

You will hear ten (10) short conversations. Each conversation is followed by one question. Choose the best answer to each question and mark the letter of the correct answer on your answer sheet. You will hear the listening ONCE.

Part 1

Listen to a biology teacher giving a lecture.

Answer question 1
1) We can infer from the talk that "Even though some animals eat human flesh, _____."

(A) there are still some humans in some primitive tribes that are man-eaters.
(B) sharks are the only man-eaters.
(C) alligators and crocodiles are the least deadliest ones.
(D) big cats don't eat human flesh.

Listen to a teacher reading an excerpt from a children's book.

Answer question 2
2) "Even though Becky was the youngest, each member of the family looked up to her" proves that _____.

(A) she was curious and wise at school.
(B) Becky taught her parents how to be respectful to others.
(C) Becky was highly respected in her family.
(D) "family" meant everything in Becky's home.

Listen to a science teacher in a science lesson.

Answer question 3
3) What is the main topic of the lesson?

(A) how to measure the speed of light
(B) the speed of light
(C) the speed of light is finite
(D) motivation of scientists

Listen to a history teacher talking to a class.

Answer question 4
4) What will the teacher probably do next?

(A) Explain the other discoverers of America
(B) Start a distinct discussion subject
(C) Describe who the Vikings were
(D) Talk about the life of Christopher Columbus

Listen to a teacher making an announcement to students.

Answer question 5
5) What is the announcement mainly about?

(A) Where and when the competition will be
(B) Students' Bulletin Board
(C) How to contact Mr. Dean
(D) How to apply for the Spelling Bee Competition

Listen to a teacher talking about a latest invention.

Answer question 6
6) What is new about this mobile phone?

(A) It is so fragile that you can damage it easily.
(B) It is not bendable.
(C) It has a transparent flexible screen.
(D) Its screen can be scratchable.

Listen to a student talking about an activity he has tried.

Answer question 7
7) What is the name of the activity?

(A) land-yatching
(B) wind-surfing
(C) sky-diving
(D) chariot swing ride

Part 1

Listen to a literature teacher in a literature class.

Answer question 8
8) According to what the teacher says, what makes a piece of writing narrative?

(A) In narrative writing, there is no need for a setting or a plot.
(B) This is a kind of writing that includes only imaginative events.
(C) Narrative writing must include fiction stories.
(D) It's a kind of writing that tells a story.

Listen to a talk about smoking.

Answer question 9
9) What can be inferred from the talk?

(A) Governments do not try hard to ban smoking, they don't care about public health.
(B) People try hard to quit smoking.
(C) However hard we try to ban people from smoking, it is hard to make them quit this habit.
(D) Health problems are not taken seriously in cultures, so they don't take precautions.

Listen to part of a lecture.

Answer question 10
10) What is the lecture mainly about?

(A) Earth's Surface
(B) The Greenhouse Effect
(C) The gases in the atmosphere
(D) Warming

You will hear a conversation between a girl and her friend. It is followed by seven questions. Choose the best answer to each question and mark the letter of the correct answer on your answer sheet. You will hear the listening ONCE.

Part 2

Listen to a boy talking to his friend and answer questions 11 to 17.

Answer question 11
11) What is the conversation mainly about?

(A) singing competition
(B) advertisements on the bulletin board
(C) school website
(D) type of music Frank likes to sing

Answer question 12
12) Where did Bill see the advertisement?

(A) in the newspaper
(B) on the school bulletin board
(C) in the school magazine
(D) on the school website

Answer question 13
13) What type of music can Fiona sing?

(A) rap
(B) opera
(C) hip hop
(D) pop

Answer question 14
14) Which of the following is true according to the conversation?

(A) Fiona can sing her pop songs.
(B) The competition is on Friday.
(C) Fiona likes singing opera.
(D) Bill is going to join the competition too.

Answer question 15
15) What time does the competition begin?

(A) at 2:30
(B) at 3 pm
(C) at 11 am
(D) 3 hours

Answer question 16
16) Where does the competition take place?

(A) at the auditorium
(B) at the leisure center
(C) in the music room
(D) at the school gym

Answer question 17
17) Fiona will probably feel _____ during the competition.

(A) great
(B) excited
(C) nervous
(D) brilliant

You will hear a conversation between two friends. It is followed by seven questions. Choose the best answer to each question and mark the letter of the correct answer on your answer sheet. You will hear the listening ONCE.

Part 3

Listen to a boy talking to his friend and answer questions 18 to 24.

Answer question 18
18) What are the speakers mainly talking about?

(A) Mrs. Abbott
(B) school assignments
(C) Tom's partner
(D) the topic of the literature assignment

Answer question 19
19) Who is David's partner on the English literature assignment?

(A) Tom
(B) Ryan
(C) Diana
(D) Jennifer

Answer question 20
20) What does Diana imply when she says; "I will be the one who will do most of the work!"

(A) She loves working alone.
(B) She believes Ryan's favorite subject is literature.
(C) She doesn't think Ryan will contribute much to the assignment.
(D) She wants to be the apple of his teacher's eye.

Answer question 21
21) What does "He never sticks to his plans" mean?

(A) He never disobeys the rules.
(B) He never keeps his promises.
(C) He keeps doing what she says.
(D) He is such a reliant person.

Answer question 22
22) According to the conversation where could Tom be?

(A) at Ryan's
(B) at the library
(C) at home
(D) at Brian's cafe

Answer question 23
23) Which of the following is true according to the conversation?

(A) David cares about Tom a lot.
(B) David is not sure whether he will finish the assignment on time.
(C) David thinks he won't be able to find Tom.
(D) Diana and David have decided to work on the assignment together.

Answer question 24
24) Why can't David check his mail?

(A) His computer is broken.
(B) He couldn't use the computers in the library.
(C) He couldn't reach Tom to use his computer.
(D) He doesn't have a computer.

You will hear a conversation between a teacher and students. It is followed by six questions. Choose the best answer to each question and mark the letter of the correct answer on your answer sheet. You will hear the listening ONCE.

Part 4

Listen to a conversation between a teacher and students then answer questions 25 to 30.

Answer question 25
25) What are the speakers mainly talking about?

(A) the Wizard Island
(B) school trip
(C) scuba diving
(D) boat tour on the lake

Answer question 26
26) What information is missing in the teacher's email?

(A) Information about the time and how they'll travel to Crater Lake
(B) Information about how the students will arrive at school
(C) Details about what they'll do during the trip
(D) Whether students should know how to swim or not

Answer question 27
27) What time do they start the trip?

(A) at 4 pm
(B) at 6 pm
(C) at 5 pm
(D) at 4:30 pm

Answer question 28
28) The_____ will pick them up.

(A) students
(B) boat trip
(C) teacher
(D) bus

Answer question 29
29) What will they do as soon as they arrive at the Lodge?

(A) go on a boat trip
(B) check-in the hotel
(C) rest for a while
(D) go to bed

Answer question 30
30) Which of the following is wrong about Crater Lake?

(A) It's the deepest lake in the U.S.
(B) It's the ninth deepest in the world.
(C) The water is crystal-clear.
(D) There are wild animals in the lake.

You will hear two students talking about Model United Nations. It is followed by five questions. Choose the best answer to each question and mark the letter of the correct answer on your answer sheet. You will hear the listening ONCE.

Part 5

Listen to two students talking and answer questions 31 to 35.

Answer question 31
31) According to the conversation, what does MUN stand for?

(A) Modern Unified Nations
(B) Modern United Nations
(C) Modernised Union Nationals
(D) More United Nations

Answer question 32
32) Which of the following is true regarding the conversation?

(A) MUN is a kind of subject that is studied in lectures.
(B) Students assume roles as delegates of different countries at MUN conferences.
(C) Mr. Abegail is the head of the MUN.
(D) International relations is not an issue of the MUN.

Answer question 33
33) What kind of skills do the participants especially show?

(A) listening skills
(B) comprehension skills
(C) reading skills
(D) negotiating and oratory skills

Answer question 34
34) According to the talk, which is not true?

(A) The aim of MUN differs from conference to conference.
(B) The MUN conferences educate participants about the workings of an international organization.
(C) High school students cannot enter the MUN conferences.
(D) The conferences broaden the view and knowledge of the students.

Answer question 35
35) The oldest modern simulation of the MUN was established _____.

(A) in 1951.
(B) by the Institution called the Hague International.
(C) by High school students.
(D) by universities.

You will hear a teacher talking about Edgar Allan Poe. It is followed by seven questions. Choose the best answer to each question and mark the letter of the correct answer on your answer sheet. You will hear the listening ONCE.

Part 6

Listen to a teacher talking about Edgar Allan Poe and then answer questions 36 to 42.

Answer question 36
36) The speaker is most probably a _____ teacher.

(A) geography
(B) literature
(C) science
(D) history

Answer question 37
37) What period did Edgar Allan Poe live in?

(A) In the eighteenth century
(B) In the early years of 1900's
(C) In the second millennium
(D) In the nineteenth century

Answer question 38
38) What was Poe's life like?

(A) His early years were full of happiness.
(B) He had a sad life.
(C) He was sorry for others' miserable lives.
(D) He enjoyed living independently.

Answer question 39
39) Who raised Poe?

(A) His readers
(B) His parents
(C) A foster family
(D) His relatives

Answer question 40
40) According to the talk, what influenced his writing?

(A) The dark side of his life
(B) Horror stories
(C) Poetry
(D) Detective stories

Answer question 41
41) Which of the following is not mentioned in the talk?

(A) He contributed a lot to the world literature.
(B) He wrote novels.
(C) He also wrote poems.
(D) He was popular with his horror stories.

Answer question 42
42) Edgar Allan Poe is still _____.

(A) worldwide popular.
(B) popular in America.
(C) living in England.
(D) loved by children.

Test 2

Paper 2: Language Form Meaning
Time: 25 Minutes
42 Questions

The Language Form and Meaning section has 42 questions. Follow along as you read the directions to the Language Form and Meaning Section.

DIRECTIONS

In this section of the test, you will finish the sentences by picking the correct word or words. The boxes contain the answers that are available to choose from. Choose the best answer to each question and mark the letter of the correct answer on your answer sheet.

Here are two sample questions:

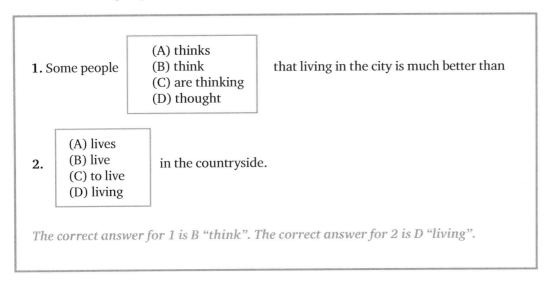

1. Some people [(A) thinks / (B) think / (C) are thinking / (D) thought] that living in the city is much better than

2. [(A) lives / (B) live / (C) to live / (D) living] in the countryside.

The correct answer for 1 is B "think". The correct answer for 2 is D "living".

Part 1

Questions 1 - 8 refer to the following email.

Dear Amy!

1. I called you today and your mom said that you
- (A) were not coming
- (B) will come
- (C) can come
- (D) may not have come

to school today.

2. I hope there isn't
- (A) everything
- (B) anything
- (C) something
- (D) nothing

serious. Will you be able to

3. attend classes tomorrow? As you know, tomorrow there
- (A) was
- (B) will be
- (C) had been
- (D) has

4. an English test
- (A) when
- (B) where
- (C) ,that
- (D) ,which

is very important. The teacher says that

5. she will not accept any
- (A) accuses
- (B) forgiveness
- (C) exceptionals
- (D) excuses

. Besides this, the teachers

6.
- (A) reserved
- (B) assigned
- (C) repeated
- (D) attained

us a lot of tasks today. Has

7. anyone from our class called and let you know
- (A) how
- (B) which
- (C) what
- (D) that

your task is?

8. If you want something, just write me back. I would be glad
- (A) to have assisted
- (B) assisting
- (C) to assist
- (D) assist

you.

Bye for now.

Your friend, Sue.

Part 2

Questions 9 - 16 refer to the following announcement.

9. Attention to all, please. Tomorrow morning all the classes are
   - (A) canceling
   - (B) be canceled
   - (C) have canceled
   - (D) canceled

10. and you
    - (A) supposed
    - (B) are supposed to
    - (C) have supposed
    - (D) are supposed be

    be in the school hall. Doctor Reynolds

11.
   - (A) is going to
   - (B) be
   - (C) is
   - (D) will be

12. give an important speech on
   - (A) will use
   - (B) to be using
   - (C) how to use
   - (D) usage

13. the internet safely. He is also going to tell us about the illnesses
   - (A) you caught
   - (B) you might catch
   - (C) you will be catching
   - (D) you to catch

14. when you are too
   - (A) few
   - (B) a little
   - (C) many
   - (D) much

   exposed to computer screens.

15. We won't accept any absenties, so please make sure
   - (A) which
   - (B) that
   - (C) where
   - (D) in that

   you come to school on time. If anyone gets sick, call the student affairs office and let

16. us
   - (A) to know
   - (B) knowing
   - (C) know
   - (D) knew

   about it.

Part 3

Questions 17 - 25 refer to the following advertisement.

17. Are you looking
- (A) for
- (B) at
- (C) on
- (D) into

something entertaining to do on the weekend?

18. Would you like
- (A) visiting
- (B) to visit
- (C) visit
- (D) to be visited

the newly-opened leisure center to experience the activities there?

19. The center,
- (A) that
- (B) where is
- (C) where
- (D) -------

located at 55 Highbury Street, is ready to offer

20.
- (A) Unfortunately,
- (B) Likewise,
- (C) For instance,
- (D) Likely,

various facilities suitable for every age group.

21. there will be art, music, language
- (A) and
- (B) however
- (C) or
- (D) but

computer

22. classes. If you want to be fit, our fitness center
- (A) may
- (B) is going
- (C) will be
- (D) be

open

23. from 9 am
- (A) between
- (B) and
- (C) to
- (D) forward

6 pm every day including weekends.

24.
- (A) Additionally,
- (B) As well as,
- (C) Apparently,
- (D) Luckily,

there will be concerts and drama shows

25.
- (A) up
- (B) at
- (C) in
- (D) on

the evenings. Please contact the number given below for further information.

Part 4

Questions 26 - 34 refer to the following letter.

Dear Mrs. Thompson,

26. 27. I am writing this letter
- (A) for apologizing
- (B) to apologize
- (C) apologizing for
- (D) apologized

to you
- (A) with the words
- (B) by my excuses
- (C) with the action
- (D) for what I did

28. in your lesson yesterday. I feel so
- (A) happy
- (B) embarrassed
- (C) enthusiastic
- (D) grateful

for my misbehavior. I really didn't mean to spoil

29. your lesson, but there were a few topics that I didn't understand while you were
- (A) talked.
- (B) talking.
- (C) had talked.
- (D) to talk.

That's why, I asked Caroline to explain those parts to me. Then you saw us talking.

30. We
- (A) were not
- (B) did not
- (C) could not
- (D) had not

trying to disrupt the lesson. I know that was not

31.
- (A) excused
- (B) expected
- (C) acceptable
- (D) acceptance

, but I am really sorry for this and I would like you

32. 33.
- (A) to accept
- (B) accept
- (C) accepting
- (D) could accept

my apology. I promise I
- (A) was going to
- (B) will
- (C) must
- (D) was

34. listen to your lessons better. I know I
- (A) will ask
- (B) had better ask
- (C) should have asked
- (D) asked

you to explain

those parts instead of asking my friend. From now on I will do my best to be the best student in the class.

Sincerely,

Pete Jefferson

Part 5

Questions 35 - 42 refer to the following e-mail.

35. Toco Toucans are different
    (A) for
    (B) from
    (C) between
    (D) then
    other birds in many ways. This bird lives in South America's

36. tropical forests and it
    (A) got used to
    (B) getting used to
    (C) used to
    (D) is used to
    living in tropical weather conditions.

37. It has a bill that is about 7.5 inch long,
    (A) which
    (B) that
    (C) where
    (D) then
    makes it special.

38.
    (A) Because
    (B) Due to
    (C) In addition
    (D) Despite
    its oversize and color, the toucan's bill has made the bird one of the world's

most popular birds.

39. By
    (A) using
    (B) use
    (C) useful
    (D) usefulness
    its bill, toucans pluck and peel fruit. Toucans

40. also use their tongues
    (A) for catch
    (B) to catch
    (C) catching
    (D) to be caught
    insects, frogs and reptiles to feed themselves.

41.
    (A) Above
    (B) In spite of
    (C) Although
    (D) What's more,
    their bills help them regulate the body temperature.

42. When they
    (A) slept
    (B) sleep
    (C) sleeping
    (D) sleeps
    , the birds tuck their bills under their feathers to keep themselves warm.

Test 2

Paper 3: Reading Comprehension
Time: 50 Minutes
42 Questions

The listening section has 42 questions. Follow along as you listen to the directions to the listening section.

DIRECTIONS

In this part of the test, you will read **five (5)** articles and then read a total of **forty-two (42)** questions. After reading the questions, pick the appropriate answer and then mark that letter on the answer sheet.

Here is a sample article.

Sample Text

> Have you ever ridden a tuk tuk? Do you know what a tuk tuk is? A tuk tuk is a three-wheeled vehicle that is used as a taxi in Bangkok. This vehicle is a kind of rickshaw that has a small engine fitted in. It is ideal for short-distant trips. As it is a very small vehicle, you don't get stuck in heavy traffic in Bangkok's busy roads. It is both convenient and cheap for commuters.

Example question 1.
3. What is this text mainly about?

(A) Means of transportation
(B) Why people prefer a tuk tuk
(C) What a tuk tuk is
(D) How to travel around Bangkok

The correct answer is *C, "What a tuk tuk is"*.

Example question 2.
4. Which one is wrong according to the text?

(A) Tuk tuks are ideal for short trips.
(B) Tuk tuks are convenient and cheap.
(C) Tuk tuks are three-wheeled.
(D) Tuk tuks are like cars with four wheels.

The correct answer is *D, "Tuk tuks are like cars with four wheels"*.

Part 1

Read the following note from the school administration and answer questions 1 - 7.

Following list shows the new schedule of tryouts for athletic teams during spring semester. Please be aware that the tryouts will be held between 16:30 and 18:30.

Short	Voleyball	Baseball	Basketball	Athleticism
Coaches in responsible	Mrs. March	Mr. Welsh	Mr. Jr. Clous	Mrs. Rogers
Time	Tues-Fri, April 3,6	Mon-Thurs, April 2,5	Mon-Tues, April 9,10	Wed-Thurs, April 11,12
Further info	Meeting will be held at the school sports hall	Meeting will be held on the baseball field	At the school basketball ring	No prior meeting

1   Unfortunately boys' soccer team has been canceled for this year. Whoever is interested in soccer, our coach, Mr. Hart is ready to train you for the following year. However, there has to be at least 11 students to participate. The school administration and the coaches have come to an agreement that both boys and girls
5   may participate in two athletic teams on condition that one should be the track team. Those who want to play more than one sports must speak with the coaches of those teams prior to tryouts. All the participants for the teams should fill in the injury release form. The deadline to hand in the form to the related coaches is two weeks before your tryouts start. Besides this form, all participants must bring a letter of
10 consent signed by the parents showing **their** approval of your participations.

1) What is the note mainly about?

(A) To inform students about the upcoming schedule for athletic events
(B) To let students learn about who will participate in the athletic teams
(C) To learn about students' preferences of athletic events
(D) To introduce the new coaches of the teams

2) Which sport will have its tryouts on April 2?

(A) Basketball
(B) Volleyball
(C) Baseball
(D) Athleticism

Part 1

3) Mr. Hart can train the students who want to play soccer only if _____ .

(A) participants take part in two sports events
(B) participants fill in a form
(C) it is in April
(D) there are 11 participants

4) Based on the passage, what is implied about the school administration and the coaches?

(A) The coaches can give decisions on their own.
(B) They work co-operatively.
(C) Both the administrators and the coaches work independently.
(D) The decisions are given by the school administrators only.

5) According to the note, what must be done before try-outs?

(A) Students must ask for an approval from the related coach
(B) Students must get permission from the school administration
(C) Students must fill in a form and bring a letter of consent signed by their parents
(D) Students must join all the try outs

6) In line 10, the word "their" refers to

(A) All the events
(B) Administrators
(C) The school coaches
(D) The parents

7) When should the students give the injury release forms to the coaches?

(A) after tryouts begin
(B) two weeks before tryouts
(C) when the coaches ask them to bring
(D) whenever they want

Part 2

Read the following email and answer questions 8 - 15.

| To : Parents of year 10 - 11 |
| From : School principal |
| Subject: End-of-school year |

1   My Dear Parents,
         Now that we have come to the last days of our school year, I'd like to start my final message by giving special thanks to all of you for your precious support that you have shown and for your participation to parent meetings the whole year.

5   This year has been a year of accomplishments. We have reached all our goals. I'd like to share some of **them** here. I'd like to start with the academic rewards. Jennifer Tomms was awarded for the state spelling bee, Robby and Judith Smith, the twins were awarded for winning the city math and science competition, and finally Julie Andrews was awarded for winning the essay writing contest.

10   Moreover, we had winning records of our athletic teams. The girls' soccer team, led by coach Angela Stevens, came in first place in the county. **This** is something that hasn't been achieved for more than 20 years. I'd like to give my special thanks to each member of the team and to our coach Angela Stevens. They worked five days a week and sometimes on the weekends by putting their heart and soul into this.

15   As summer begins soon, let me remind you that students must complete their summer reading. I've enclosed the list of books that should be read. All students must choose at least 10 books from the list and after reading the books we want them to write short reports or reviews on the books they have read.
         Finally, the end-of-school party will be held in the school hall Friday 4th, starting at 4 pm.

20   Student lockers should have been cleaned out before 3 pm on that day.
         I wish you all a good summer vacation. I will always be willing to help whenever you have any concerns about the school or about your child.

Sincerely,
Bart Brian
Principal

[Send]

8) What is the main reason for the principal writing this email to the parents?

(A) To get their remarks about the school
(B) To invite them to school
(C) To give his end-of-school day remarks
(D) To discuss the school problems

Part 2

9) In line 5, the word "accomplishments" is closest in meaning to ....

(A) achievements
(B) access
(C) experiences
(D) acceptances

10) In line 6, the word "them" refers to ....

(A) the participants
(B) the accomplishments
(C) the sport events
(D) the administrators

11) According to the email, which of the following is not true?

(A) It is the last days of the education year.
(B) Some students won awards from competitions.
(C) All the students received academic awards.
(D) The principal appreciates the parents' support.

12) In line 11, the word "this" refers to ....

(A) the girl's soccer team's success
(B) the entire state
(C) the coach, Angela Stevens
(D) girls' soccer team

13) Which of the following is wrong regarding the girls' soccer team?

(A) It was led by coach Angela Stevens.
(B) The team came in first place in the county.
(C) The team's success hasn't been achieved for more than 20 years in the city.
(D) The principal thinks their success hasn't been appreciated well enough.

14) In line 14, the idiom "put their heart and soul into" is closest in meaning to ....

(A) try and make an effort
(B) work independently
(C) succeed without any help
(D) put their heads together

15) Which of the following doesn't exist in the principal's last words?

(A) summer vacation assignments
(B) books that will be read in summer
(C) student lockers to be cleaned out
(D) summer school camp

Part 3

Read the passage and answer questions 16 - 22.

1   Expeditions started in the early years of the fifteenth century and lasted for two following centuries. Many European explorers set sail on their journeys to undiscovered destinations. Francis Drake was one of the most prominent adventurers of his time, because he accomplished a number of **feats of bravery** that gained
5   respect in his society as he was fearless and bold. That is to say, he was highly **esteemed** by his folks. He was a navigator, a politician, a slave trader and a privateer. He participated in the earliest English slaving voyages to Africa.
      Following the years when Columbus discovered **the New World**, the Spanish started to set colonies there, where they had a great amount of treasure.
10   Queen Elizabeth I assigned Sir Francis Drake and his cousin, John Hawkins to capture the treasure of Spain. So they set off to accomplish this duty. The queen hoped to put an end to the Anglo-Spanish War. Sir Francis Drake and his cousin defeated the Spanish and captured the treasure. This made him a wealthy man, and the Queen rewarded him with a knighthood in 1581. By **then**, he was considered the
15   bravest sailor in England.
    The war broke out between England and Spain four years later. In 1588, King Philip II of Spain sent a fleet to defeat England. Drake, second in command of the army of England gained victory against the Spanish army.
      Sir Francis Drake is known for being the second Explorer to circumnavigate the
20   globe after Ferdinand Magellan. He died off the coast of Panama in 1596 and was buried at sea.

16) What is the passage mainly about?

(A) The Age of Exploration
(B) Sir Francis Drake and his accomplishments
(C) The treasure of Spain
(D) The acts of Queen Elizabeth

17) In line 4, the phrase feats of bravery is closest in meaning to _____.

(A) Acts of great courage
(B) Self-confidence
(C) Adventurousness
(D) Strong determination

18) In line 6, the word esteemed means _____

(A) admired
(B) adored
(C) beloved
(D) respected

Part 3

19) What does the author mean by "the New World"?

(A) American continent
(B) Undiscovered destination
(C) European countries
(D) Central Europe

20) Why did Queen Elizabeth assign Drake and his cousin to set sail to the New World?

(A) to invade Spain
(B) to capture Spanish treasure
(C) to be dominant in the New World
(D) to establish colonies

21) In line 14, the word then refers to _____

(A) three years after the war
(B) the year when the war broke out
(C) the time he was knighted by the queen
(D) the year 1585

22) According to the passage, which of the following is not mentioned about Francis Drake?

(A) the time he was knighted by the queen
(B) when he defeated the Spanish army
(C) his early childhood
(D) as he was the second man to circumnavigate the world

Part 4

Read the article and answer questions 23 - 31.

1   Pollution causes many damages in nature. Acid rain, in other words; acid precipitation is one of **them**. It is a result of air pollution. Any form of **precipitation** from the atmosphere with acidic components falling to the ground results in acid rain. These acidic components are sulfuric or nitric.

5   When sulfur dioxide and nitrogen oxides are emitted and transported by wind, acid rain falls onto the ground. In fact, rain is usually acidic due to the oxides that naturally exist in the air. Unpolluted rain has a pH value of 5 or 6. On the other hand, acid rain polluted with nitrogen oxides and sulphur dioxide has a pH value of 4, or in some cases it has a pH value of 2. Acidity is measured with the pH scale. The lower the pH

10   value of the air has, the more acidic the rain is, which means while "0" is the most acidic, "14" is the most alkaline (opposite of acidic).

         In reality, acid rain is not as harmful to humans as it is thought. When human skin is exposed to contaminated water- water that is polluted with harmful gases or minerals- there won't be a health risk. However, when the gases that cause acid rain

15   (nitrogen oxides, sulfur oxides) are inhaled by human beings, respiratory diseases are **inevitable**.

         In order to stop acid rain, governments should work cooperatively and take legal precautions to reduce emissions that cause acid rain. For instance, renewable energy must be expanded, the use of fosil fuels has to be reduced. Unless any

20   precautions are taken, not only acid rain will affect human beings, all living things and the environment will be widely damaged.

23) Which <u>title</u> best summarizes the article?

(A) Acid rain and its effects
(B) Harmful gases
(C) Causes of deaths
(D) Harsh conditions

24) In line 2, <u>them</u> refers to _____ .

(A) acid rain
(B) disasters
(C) damages
(D) causes

25) Which of the following statements does paragraph 1 include?

(A) Air pollution causes acid rain.
(B) The most damaging pollution is caused by acid rain.
(C) Pollution is the biggest problem of the world.
(D) There are some ways to avoid acid rain.

Part 4

26) In line 2, the word <u>precipitation</u> can be replaced with _____.

(A) damage
(B) shower
(C) rainfall
(D) resistance

27) What is paragraph 2 <u>mainly</u> about?

(A) What causes acid rains
(B) How the acidity of rain is measured
(C) How to protect ourselves from air pollution
(D) Effects of acid rains

28) Which of the following is <u>true</u> regarding the pH values according to the text?

(A) The pH value of "0" symbolizes the least acidic value.
(B) As the pH value falls, the acidic value of the air gets lower.
(C) As the pH value increases, the acidic ratio decreases.
(D) The higher the pH value gets, the more acidic the air is.

29) Which of the following is <u>true</u> according to paragraph 3?

(A) Human skin is very sensitive when exposed to acid rain.
(B) Inhaling the poisonous gases causes health problems.
(C) Acid rain is not at all risky for our nature.
(D) The gases that cause acid rain are not poisonous.

30) In line 16, the word <u>inevitable</u> means _____.

(A) inescapable
(B) unmanageable
(C) infectious
(D) destructive

31) Which paragraph tells us about the measures to prevent acid rain?

(A) 1
(B) 3
(C) 4
(D) 5

Part 5

Read the text and answer questions 32 - 37.

1   Some of the most distinct ecosystems in the world are Coral Reefs. **They** house millions of marine species. Coral reefs are protrusions that are alike rocks made from corals. Corals are marine invertebrate animals that belong to a large group of colorful and fascinating animals called Cnidaria.

5   Unlike mammals, amphibians, reptiles, fish and birds which have vertebrae, marine invertebrates don't have backbones. They are ancient animals that are related to jellyfish and anemones. An individual coral is called a polyp, which extends its tentacles at night to ingest tiny organisms, planktons and other small creatures to feed itself. Thousands of identical polyps live together and form a coral colony.

10   There are couple of reasons of why many sea creatures, **especially** small fish live in coral reefs. One of them is that the reefs are rich in nutrients. There is a plenty of food for them to ingest. The other reason is that coral reefs are secure places for them to keep them away from large predators. For instance, big sharks can be hurt from the hard rocky reefs, which are some of the most dangerous predators for such small fish.

15   Unfortunately, coral reefs are in danger of extinction due to natural and man-made reasons. The most important natural reason is that the temperature of the water in oceans is not stable where coral reefs exist. The temperature of the water may be too hot or too cold because of many reasons. However, coral reefs require ideal conditions in order to survive. They can only live in warm waters, so they mostly exist in tropical areas.

20   Considering man-made reasons, pollution is the most important impact on the loss of coral reefs. Dumping chemicals and rubbish in the waters can destroy coral reefs because they are very sensitive and fragile. Besides this, fishermen use dynamites while fishing. While they are killing numerous fish, these explosives damage the reefs in the process as well.

25   In addition to all man-made damages, cutting off coral from reefs to make jewelry is the most pathetic one.

32) In line 1, the word "they" refers to _____

(A) Mammals
(B) Coral reefs
(C) Ecosystems
(D) Marine species

33) According to the text, what do protrusions look like?

(A) Rocks made from corals
(B) Invertebrate animals
(C) Polyps
(D) Small creatures

Part 5

34) According to the text, which of the following is not true?

(A) Mammals and amphibians are vertebrates.
(B) Polyps use their tentacles for feeding.
(C) Marine invertebrates don't have backbones.
(D) An individual coral is called an anemone.

35) In line 10, the word "especially" can be replaced by _____ .

(A) definitely
(B) chiefly
(C) only
(D) inexceptionally

36) Why do many sea creatures like fish live in coral reefs?

(A) Coral reefs are safe and rich in nutrients.
(B) There are sharks in the deep waters of oceans.
(C) Coral reefs face the danger of extinction.
(D) There is enough sun-exposure in the shallow waters for coral reefs to survive.

37) Which of the following is not one of the man-made reasons of the extinction of coral reefs?

(A) The explosures that fishermen use while fishing destroy coral reefs.
(B) The sea temperature in the oceans constantly changes.
(C) Dumping chemicals and rubbish into the waters damage coral reefs.
(D) To make jewelery some people cut off coral from reefs.

Part 6

Read the passage and answer questions 38 - 42.

1   What is Venus like? People have always been curious about planets. Over the years, numbers of theories concerning whether there is life on planets, and how they were formed have risen among science people. It has always **captured the imaginations of** them.

5   Venus is the second planet from the sun. **It** is named for the Roman goddess of love. It is the only planet that was named after a female. This makes it unique. In ancient times, Venus was thought to be two distinct stars, one of which appeared at sunset and the other appeared at sunrise. They were named as Vesper and Lucifer. The **latter** became known as the name of Satan later on.

10   Although Venus is not the closest planet to the sun, it is the hottest one. The reason for this is that heat is trapped by its dense atmosphere. To be more specific, temperatures on Venus can reach up to 900 degrees Fahrenheit, which equals to about 480 degrees Celcius. Despite its hellish atmosphere, it is thought by the scientists that Venus may once have been habitable.

15   Scientists are constantly looking for signs of life. Although lots of probes have been sent to Venus, none have found a trace of life. Here on our planet, the surface pressure is ideal for us to survive. On the other hand, it is completely different on Venus. The surface pressure has an adverse effect on any kind of living being to survive.

20   Furthermore, Venus has strong winds that blow at around 450 miles an hour. What will happen in the future is still a mystery. One day scientists may find life on other planets. Who knows?

38) What is the best title for the passage?

(A) The hottest planet
(B) Important research
(C) Is there life on Venus
(D) The universe

39) In line 3, we can use the word _____ instead of the idiom "captured the imagination of".

(A) distracted
(B) fascinated
(C) imagined
(D) discouraged

Part 6

40) In line 5, the word <u>it</u> refers to _____.

(A) the sun
(B) planet
(C) Venus
(D) goddess of love

41) In line 9, the word "latter" can be replaced by _____.

(A) lately
(B) previously
(C) first one
(D) last-mentioned

42) Which paragraphs show that life on Venus may not be possible for living beings?

(A) 1-2
(B) Only 2
(C) 3-4-5
(D) None

Section 2
PRACTICE TEST 3

Test 3

Paper 3: Listening Comprehension
Time: 40 Minutes
42 Questions

The listening section has 42 questions. Follow along as you listen to the directions to the listening section.

DIRECTIONS

In this section of the test, you will hear conversations, announcements or instructions. Each conversation, announcement or instruction is followed by one question. Choose the best answer to each question and mark the letter of the correct answer on your answer sheet. You will hear each conversation, announcement or instruction only one time. You will have enough time to transfer your answers from the question paper to the answer sheet at the end of the listening section.

Here is an example:

What does the woman mean?

(A) She will attend the meeting soon.
(B) She will have to miss the meeting.
(C) She thinks she will not be invited to the meeting.
(D) She has to be somewhere else at the time of the meeting.

The correct answer is *(B), "She will have to miss the meeting."*

Here is another example:

What are the speakers talking about?

(A) Their summer time activites
(B) Going on a vacation
(C) Spring festival
(D) An upcoming test

The correct answer is *(C), "Spring festival".*

Go on to the next page, and the test will begin with question number one.

Audio recordings of this section can be accessed by scanning this QR code on your device

You will hear ten (10) short conversations. Each conversation is followed by one question. Choose the best answer to each question and mark the letter of the correct answer on your answer sheet. You will hear the listening ONCE.

Part 1

Listen to a math teacher giving a lecture.

Answer question 1
1) We can infer from the talk that Pi _____.

(A) is proved to be rational.
(B) has been studied since the ancient times.
(C) should be studied theoretically.
(D) was first discovered in 1882.

Listen to a language teacher reading an excerpt from a story book.

Answer question 2
2) According to the story what may be the gift that a snowman leaves when it melts?

(A) tree roots
(B) flowers
(C) crystals
(D) water

Listen to a class teacher.

Answer question 3
3) What is the primary reason for the teacher making this announcement?

(A) to tell students what friendship means
(B) to ask them to support the school authority
(C) to get students' ideas about "Help a Friend Day"
(D) to make students understand the value of encouragement

Listen to a principal talking to students.

Answer question 4
4) According to the announcement how was Roxanne nominated to represent the school in the Mental Maths Competitions?

(A) by students' votes
(B) unanimously by teachers' votes
(C) by the principal
(D) because of her success at school

Listen to a principal making an announcement.

Answer question 5
5) According to the announcement what does the principal mean with "inclement weather"?

(A) gloomy weather with dark clouds
(B) cool but nice weather
(C) mild weather conditions
(D) severe, stormy weather with rains

Part 1

Listen to a teacher talking to a student.

Answer question 6
6) Why does the teacher suggest that Tina write for the school newspaper? Which of the following reasons may not be the reason?

(A) Because the teacher believes that she is gifted.
(B) Because she got the highest mark.
(C) Because her writing is wonderful.
(D) The teacher thinks she can make her writing skills better by doing that.

Listen to a teacher talking to a student.

Answer question 7
7) What will the teacher probably do next?

(A) cancel the project
(B) write a report to the school authority
(C) try to convince the student's mother
(D) go on with the project without the student

Listen to a girl.

Answer question 8
8) What does the girl imply about John?

(A) He must continue with his studies.
(B) He must be punished for his wrongdoings.
(C) He shouldn't attend Mr.Harvey's lessons any more.
(D) He should apologize to the teacher.

Listen to a head teacher's announcement.

Answer question 9
9) Which of the following is not mentioned in the announcement?

(A) How far the ride will be
(B) Starting point and time of the ride
(C) What to wear
(D) Who will participate

Listen to a school counsellor giving some advice to a student.

Answer question 10
10) Why does the student need some advice?

(A) Because he needs to speak to his chemistry teacher.
(B) Because he wants to do an experiment in the lab.
(C) Because his chemistry exam results are very low.
(D) Because he wants to work in the lab.

You will hear a conversation between a boy and his friend. It is followed by six questions. Choose the best answer to each question and mark the letter of the correct answer on your answer sheet. You will hear the listening ONCE.

Listen to a boy talking to his friend and answer questions 11 to 16.

Answer question 11
11) What is the main purpose of Brian talking to Jennifer?

(A) to invite Jennifer to go to the new mall
(B) to talk about Jennifer's sister
(C) to ask Jennifer about life in Europe
(D) to ask Jennifer where his sister lives

Answer question 12
12) Why can't Jennifer join her friends?

(A) She will be flying to London.
(B) She will spend the day with her parents.
(C) She will pick up her sister from the airport.
(D) She's flying to visit her sister in London.

Answer question 13
13) Which of the following is not mentioned about Jennifer's sister?

(A) She is flying from England to visit her family.
(B) She is attending the Royal Academy of Music.
(C) She is thinking of living in England in the future.
(D) She is doing her masters degree in UK at the moment.

Answer question 14
14) Which of the following is true according to the conversation?

(A) Brian and Jennifer are planning to share a flat when they go to university.
(B) Brian wants to study abroad.
(C) Jennifer is going to join her friends in the afternoon.
(D) Jennifer is going to visit her friend on the following day.

Answer question 15
15) According to the conversation what is mainly compared between America and Europe?

(A) The hectic life
(B) The lifestyles
(C) The people
(D) The weather

Answer question 16
16) What does Jennifer mean by saying " It may be weird to adopt to a new life, but then you'll get used to it."?

(A) Her friend will get accustomed to the new life in time.
(B) Her friend has difficulty in getting used to the new lifestyle.
(C) Her friend finds the new lifestyle hard to get used to.
(D) She will help her friend how to deal with the difficulties in getting accustomed to the new lifestyle.

You will hear a conversation between two friends. It is followed by six questions. Choose the best answer to each question and mark the letter of the correct answer on your answer sheet. You will hear the listening ONCE.

Part 3

Listen to a boy talking to his friend and answer questions 17 to 22.

Answer question 17
17) What are the speakers mainly talking about?

(A) Mr. Black
(B) the school board
(C) the science fair
(D) the rules

Answer question 18
18) How may James probably feel when he hears about the science fair from Donna?

(A) annoyed
(B) excited
(C) relieved
(D) serious

Answer question 19
19) According to the conversation which of the following is not mentioned about the science fair?

(A) When it will be held
(B) What the school administrators think about it
(C) Who organised it
(D) How many schools have been invited

Answer question 20
20) Why is Donna the only student who knows about the fair?

(A) Because she has been working on an experiment with Mr. Black.
(B) Because her father is the head of the commission.
(C) Because her teacher told her not to mention it to anyone.
(D) Because she is the only one that can take part in such competitions.

Answer question 21
21) According to the conversation which of the following is not true?

(A) There'll be more than one competition.
(B) There'll be two kinds of competitions.
(C) The commission to decide on the participants involves science teachers.
(D) Individual participants don't take part in the competitions.

Answer question 22
22) Which of the following is true according to the conversation?

(A) James and Donna will participate in the competitions together.
(B) Donna offers James to help him with his project.
(C) Donna will not take part in the team competitions.
(D) James decides to work on a project, too.

> You will hear a conversation between two fellow students. It is followed by six questions. Choose the best answer to each question and mark the letter of the correct answer on your answer sheet. You will hear the listening ONCE.

Part 4

Listen to two fellow students and answer questions 23 to 28.

Answer question 23
23) What are the students mainly talking about?

(A) why they are so busy at school
(B) why parents are very strict
(C) activities at school
(D) why teachers are so lenient

Answer question 24
24) According to the conversation, what cannot be inferred about extracurricular activities?

(A) activities that are outside the regular academic curriculum
(B) activities that students need to do in order to get more credit
(C) activities that are not part of the course or study
(D) activities that take place outside the normal school timetable

Answer question 25
25) What does Susan imply about her extracurricular activities?

(A) She loves being occupied with loads of work.
(B) She is thinking about doing only one of them.
(C) She thinks they take too much of her time.
(D) She is thinking of reconsidering them.

Answer question 26
26) Her busiest extracurricular activity is _____.

(A) The school assignments
(B) The school yearbook committee
(C) Exams at school
(D) The school newspaper

Answer question 27
27) Which of the following is true according to what she says about her activities?

(A) She writes more than one article for the newspaper each week.
(B) Writing for the newspaper takes more time than working for the yearbook committee.
(C) She doesn't enjoy doing any of the extracurricular activities.
(D) The school yearbook committee members have meetings twice or three times a week.

Answer question 28
28) What does Robert mean by saying; "Your schedule is really packed."?

(A) You have a busy agenda.
(B) You don't seem very busy.
(C) Your programme is ready.
(D) You always stick to your plan.

You will hear a gemologist talking about gem stones. It is followed by five questions. Choose the best answer to each question and mark the letter of the correct answer on your answer sheet. You will hear the listening ONCE.

Part 5

Listen to the talk and answer questions 29 to 33.

Answer question 29
29) What do gemologists <u>mainly</u> study?

(A) beads
(B) gem stones
(C) jewelery
(D) lime stone

Answer question 30
30) "Some gem stones are believed to have special powers." is similar in meaning to _____

(A) Gem stones are thought to be unreal.
(B) Some consider gem stones to be magical.
(C) Some think that gem stones carry peculiar powers.
(D) Gem stones are considered to be out of this world.

Answer question 31
31) Which of the following does the student <u>not mention</u> about his mom?

(A) She collects minerals and stones.
(B) She has a range of colored stones.
(C) She has a variety of stones from all over the world.
(D) She herself is a gemologist.

Answer question 32
32) The word "specimen" can be replaced by _____.

(A) indication
(B) similar
(C) sample
(D) variety

Answer question 33
33) Which of the following is <u>not true</u> according to the professor's talk?

(A) Gemologists identify, grade and certify the quality of gem stones.
(B) All diamonds are formed deep underground the earth.
(C) The places where diamonds are found near the surface of the earth are volcanic areas.
(D) Volcanic activity forces diamonds to the surface.

You will hear a science teacher talking to a class. It is followed by four questions. Choose the best answer to each question and mark the letter of the correct answer on your answer sheet. You will hear the listening ONCE.

Part 6

Listen to a science teacher talking to a class and then answer questions 34 to 37.

Answer question 34
34) What is the main subject of the lesson?

(A) the solar system
(B) the moon
(C) moons
(D) formation of the earth

Answer question 35
35) Which of the following is not true according to the talk?

(A) The solar system is made up of the sun and planets, asteroids, moons, comets and meteroids.
(B) Moons are the small objects that orbit the sun indirectly.
(C) Planets are the objects that orbit the sun indirectly.
(D) Mercury is the smallest planet.

Answer question 36
36) What does the word "Sol" stand for?

(A) the Solar System
(B) the Sun
(C) moons
(D) the Earth

Answer question 37
37) Which of the following is in the inner solar system?

(A) Venus
(B) Saturn
(C) Uranus
(D) Neptune

You will hear a literature talking about George Orwell. It is followed by five questions. Choose the best answer to each question and mark the letter of the correct answer on your answer sheet. You will hear the listening ONCE.

Part 7

Listen to a literature teacher talking about George Orwell and then answer questions 38 to 42.

Answer question 38
38) We learn from the talk that _____.

(A) George Orwell was not the real name of the writer.
(B) George Orwell wrote about his own experiences.
(C) George Orwell was popular only in his country.
(D) George Orwell lived a long life.

Answer question 39
39) According to the talk, he made an awareness of social injustice, and he opposed _____

(A) justice
(B) democracy
(C) totalitarianism
(D) socialism

Answer question 40
40) George Orwell's interest in literature started _____.

(A) in 1950.
(B) at his early ages.
(C) after he started school.
(D) when his father was in India.

Answer question 41
41) What is one of the reasons why George developed strange habits like talking to imaginary characters?

(A) He grew up in a solitary life.
(B) His parents were not close to him.
(C) He was isolated at school by the teachers.
(D) He was the middle child of three.

Answer question 42
42) Which of the following is wrong about George Orwell and his works?

(A) "Animal Farm" and "Nineteen Eighty-Four" are George Orwell's most popular works.
(B) There are political issues in both novels; "Animal Farm" and "Nineteen Eighty-Four".
(C) "Shooting an Elephant" by George Orwell was turned into a film.
(D) "Nineteen Eighty-Four" was George Orwell's masterpiece.

Test 3

Paper 2: Language Form And Meaning
Time: 25 Minutes
42 Questions

The Language Form and Meaning section has 42 questions. Follow along as you read the directions to the Language Form and Meaning Section.

DIRECTIONS

In this section of the test, you will finish the sentences by picking the correct word or words. The boxes contain the answers that are available to choose from. Choose the best answer to each question and mark the letter of the correct answer on your answer sheet.

Here are two sample question:

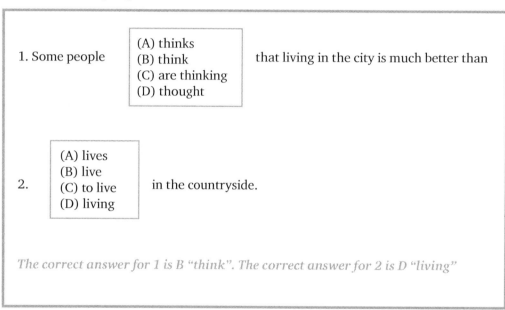

1. Some people [(A) thinks / (B) think / (C) are thinking / (D) thought] that living in the city is much better than

2. [(A) lives / (B) live / (C) to live / (D) living] in the countryside.

The correct answer for 1 is B "think". The correct answer for 2 is D "living"

Part 1

Questions 1 - 6 refer to the following e-mail.

Dear Mr. Smith,

1. I am sorry that I
- (A) have missed
- (B) missed
- (C) couldn't miss
- (D) had missed

the lesson on Monday. My father had an

2. operation and I
- (A) may have stayed
- (B) must stay
- (C) had to stay
- (D) had stayed

with him in the hospital. My mom called the

3. school office to tell them
- (A) about
- (B) for
- (C) into
- (D) with

it. I wanted to let you know, too. Today he's

4. feeling
- (A) most
- (B) much
- (C) by far
- (D) less

better, so I will come to school soon. Melinda told

5. me that you gave me an extension on the homework. I'd like
- (A) thank
- (B) thanking
- (C) to thank
- (D) to have thanked

6. you for your
- (A) considered.
- (B) consider.
- (C) consideration.
- (D) have considered.

Kind Regards,

Louise

Part 2

Questions 7 - 10 refer to the following message.

To: Students of class 10C

From: Mr. Blink

7. The writing assignment I gave on Tuesday doesn't have
   - (A) to do
   - (B) to be done
   - (C) to have been done
   - (D) doing

8. until the end of next week. You may write up
   - (A) from
   - (B) least
   - (C) to
   - (D) at

   150 words for your

9. essay. Anyone
   - (A) who
   - (B) ever
   - (C) what
   - (D) whatever

   needs help can find me in my office. I

10. will be working in my office all day from 10 am
    - (A) for
    - (B) up
    - (C) to
    - (D) and

5 pm next week, so don't hesitate to visit me for further questions.

You can also e-mail me: h.Blink63@gmail.com

Thank you.

Part 2

Questions 11 - 16 refer to the following e-mail.

Dear Mathew,

11. I am looking forward to
 (A) graduating
 (B) will graduate
 (C) graduate
 (D) would graduate
from university. I still have one

12. year to go. On one hand, I'm a bit
 (A) nervous
 (B) enthusiastic
 (C) fearful
 (D) thrilling

13. that I am about to finish my school life.
 (A) On the other hand,
 (B) Besides,
 (C) Furthermore,
 (D) In addition,

14. I feel a bit scared, because everything
 (A) will be
 (B) was
 (C) has been
 (D) would
different in my life.

15. I will miss all my friends in my class,
 (A) so
 (B) because
 (C) but
 (D) and so
we

16. have shared
 (A) for
 (B) as
 (C) such
 (D) so
many things together, but you know everything

has an end.

Anyway, when I graduate I am planning to move back to Miami. What about your plans?

Get in touch soon.

Mark.

Part 3

Questions 17 - 22 refer to the following e-mail.

17. The school drama club is pleased [(A) presenting / (B) to have presented / (C) to present / (D) presenting] the play "The

18. Tempest". The play will [(A) be performed / (B) performing / (C) performs / (D) perform] next week during the Shakespeare Schools' Festival.

As you know the Shakespeare Schools' Festival has

19. the [(A) well-known / (B) popular / (C) famous / (D) reputation] of being the world's largest youth drama festival.

20. This year there will be more [(A) from / (B) to / (C) as / (D) than] 20,000 students across from the US. Our school's

performance will be on August, 3. Tickets cost $ 4,00 and can be

21. [(A) sold / (B) buying / (C) purchased / (D) sale] from the Student Affairs Office or you may get them at the

22. door [(A) previous / (B) prior / (C) former / (D) ahead] to the play. We will be happy to see all of you at the performance.

Part 4

Questions 23 - 30 refer to the following advertisement.

Dear Diary,

23. I'm so excited now,
 (A) so
 (B) because
 (C) therefore
 (D) besides
today's the first day of our Paris school

24. trip. I can't wait for tomorrow's field trip to visit the Palais Garnier,
 (A) which
 (B) by what
 (C) where
 (D) whose

25. is the magnificent opera house of Paris. The building
 (A) considering
 (B) considers
 (C) consider
 (D) is considered

26. to be an architectural masterpiece.
 (A) It is
 (B) It has
 (C) Its
 (D) It's
construction started in 1861

27. and finished in 1875 at the request
 (A) from
 (B) of
 (C) in
 (D) at
Napoleon III. They say it

28. is one of the most dazzling
 (A) structure
 (B) monuments
 (C) landmark
 (D) constructions
in Paris. Mr. Dianason,

29. our drama teacher said that we
 (A) would be taken
 (B) will take
 (C) are taking
 (D) are being taken
to the theater boxes on the 1st floor and also see

the backstage where the opera singers, actors and actresses get ready for their performance.

30. I am looking forward
 (A) at
 (B) by
 (C) to
 (D) into
this trip.

I don't know how I will be able to sleep tonight.

Part 6

Questions 31 - 36 refer to the following magazine article.

31. The
(A) developing
(B) develop
(C) developed
(D) development
of writing made a huge difference to the world. Hieroglyphics and other forms of "picture writing" developed around Mesopotamia, where

32. the Sumerian civilization
(A) was
(B) has
(C) to be
(D) has been
based. The first accurate alphabet was used by the Phoenicians around 1050 BC. That alphabet had 22 letters and was used for more than 1000 years. The modern European alphabet is based on the Greek.

33. A number of changes took
(A) place
(B) part
(C) control
(D) account
as time passed.

34. The Romans
(A) divided
(B) added
(C) instructed
(D) appeared
the letter G. The letters J and V

35. were unknown
(A) along
(B) to
(C) at
(D) with
people in Shakespeare's time.

36. If we
(A) hold up
(B) make off
(C) bring on
(D) look into
the history of writing in more detail, we will find interesting facts.

Part 7

Questions 37 - 42 refer to the following article.

37. Kibasen,
    (A) other saying
    (B) in other words
    (C) someone calls
    (D) by means of
    "Cavalry Battle", is a kind of riding sport which

38. is played in Japan. It's
    (A) plays
    (B) playing
    (C) played
    (D) has been played
    by children. They play this

39. during their annual sports day. There can be as
    (A) much
    (B) many
    (C) not
    (D) few
    teams as

40. possible. The players of
    (A) each
    (B) all of
    (C) every of
    (D) many
    team wear bandanas in different colors. These

bandanas play an important role in the game, because if someone from the opponent team grabs one of the

41. players' bandana, the team of that player loses the game and is
    (A) rejoins
    (B) enters
    (C) dismissed
    (D) eliminated
    . The game is played

on large fields and there are four players, three of which are on the ground, one player rides on top of the three

42. players. The game
    (A) starts
    (B) move on
    (C) goes on
    (D) continue
    until all the teams in the field are eliminated except one, the winner.

Test 3

Paper 3: Reading Comprehension
Time: 50 Minutes
42 Questions

DIRECTIONS

In this part of the test, you will read five (5) articles and then read a total of forty-two (42) questions. After reading the questions, pick the appropriate answer and then mark that letter in the answer sheet.

Here is a sample article.

Sample Text

> Have you ever ridden a tuk tuk? Do you know what a tuk tuk is? A tuk tuk is a three-wheeled vehicle that is used as a taxi in Bangkok. This vehicle is a kind of rickshaw that has a small engine fitted in. It is ideal for short-distant trips. As it is a very small vehicle, you don't get stuck in heavy traffic in Bangkok's busy roads. It is both convenient and cheap for commuters.

Example question 1.
5. What is this text mainly about?

(I) Means of transportation
(J) Why people prefer tuk tuk
(K) What a tuk tuk is
(L) How to travel around Bangkok

The correct answer is *C, "What a tuk tuk is"*.

Example question 2.
6. Which one is wrong according to the text?

(I) Tuk tuks are ideal for short trips.
(J) Tuk tuks are convenient and cheap.
(K) Tuk tuks are three-wheeled.
(L) Tuk tuks are like cars with four wheels.

The correct answer is *D, "Tuk tuks are like cars with four wheels"*.

Part 1

Read the following announcement made by a principal and answer questions 1 - 7.

A schedule for the school's newest elective courses was released on our web site last Wednesday. Here we would like to inform all of you about these courses thinking that some of you may not have checked our web site yet. Please look at the list and take notes, especially if you are thinking of joining one of the elective courses. As you will see, there are certain meeting times for each course. Try not to miss that, because whoever doesn't attend the initial meeting of the course will not be registered. The consultants' names for the courses are given in the list, so for further questions please apply to the relevant teacher.

Elective Courses	Consultants	Meeting Time	Objectives of the course
International Marketing	Jonathan Coll	Thursday, 2 pm	Learn about international business and marketing strategies
Web-design	Sue Smith	Thursday, 2 pm	Learn how to create web-sites
Further info	Emmy Hensinsky	Friday, 11 am	Learn about public health issues
Economy	Amanda Trailer	Friday, 3 pm	Learn about public health issues

1) Who is this announcement most probably for?

(A) The students who are already registered to courses
(B) The faculty consultants
(C) The students who may not have checked the school's web page
(D) The students who have just got registered

2) What's the main purpose of the schedule?

(A) To mention some of the clubs that will start the following year
(B) To advise students on which elective courses to join
(C) To let students know about their faculty consultants
(D) To make students aware of the recent elective courses

Part 1

3) Who does the principal refer to when he says that students should take notes while looking at the list?

(A) The students who already attend the elective courses
(B) The students who want to join one of the elective courses
(C) All the students of the school
(D) The new graduates

4) What will happen if a student doesn't attend the initial meeting?

(A) He won't be registered to the courses.
(B) He will be dismissed.
(C) He will be punished.
(D) He will have to talk to his advisor.

5) Which elective course should a student join if he / she is interested in using the internet?

(A) International Marketing
(B) Economy
(C) Public Health
(D) Web-design

6) What can be inferred from the content of the elective course on economy?

(A) It will be useful for students to learn how to manage their budget.
(B) It will deal with global issues.
(C) It will teach students international techniques.
(D) Students will benefit from modern techniques.

(7) According to the table, all the meetings are in the afternoon, EXCEPT FOR _____ .

(A) International Marketing
(B) Economy
(C) Public Health
(D) Web-design

Part 2

Read the following e-mail and answer questions 8 - 15.

New Message

To	: Students of Year 11
From	: Bart Enders
Subject:	Evaluation Criteria

Line,

1   Here is what you are expected to do in the literature class this semester. Please pay attention to my words very carefully.

   I'll give you 4 reading assignments. I'll expect you to prepare a talk about each of the reading topics so that you can involve in the class debates. Your participation in these class
5   debates will be evaluated out of twenty percent of your total grade. Furthermore, you will be given 2-page writting assignments on a topic we will be studying. These will be graded at the end of each week (30% of your average mark will contribute to your end-of-year grade). We will apply five tests during the semester. Each of them will be worth 10 percent of your final grade. You may be called on during class to check what you have done so far.
10   When I call on you, try to answer my questions correctly, as they will help you get bonus marks. I want all of you to try hard in my class. You have to be ready at all times. What I mean is, you should work regulary. Furthermore, you will be given an outline of the material. I wish you a successful semester. For anything that you don't understand, get in touch with me.

Send

8) *What is the massage mainly about?*

(A) How the teacher evaluates students' exams
(B) The teacher's advice on how to study out of the class
(C) The type of homework the students will do in class
(D) What the teacher expects from the students in his class this semester

9) *Based on the message, what is probably not true about the students' reading assignments?*

(A) The grade that they will receive from these assignments will not affect the final grade.
(B) They are worth a small percentage of the students' final grade.
(C) The students are expected to prepare a talk about each reading topic.
(D) The students will not be given more than four reading assignments.

Part 2

10) In line 4, which of the following word can be used instead of "debate"?

(A) speech
(B) row
(C) discussion
(D) chat

11) In line 4, what does "these" refer to?

(A) class debates
(B) students' participations
(C) assignments
(D) students' grades

12) Which of the following is not mentioned in the message about something that the students will be graded on?

(A) homework assignments
(B) attendance
(C) tests
(D) class participation

13) In line 11, the phrasal verb "call on" can be replaced by _____.

(A) call upon
(B) call after
(C) call for
(D) call away

14) In line 11, the phrase "at all times" can be replaced by _____.

(A) at the time
(B) sometimes
(C) always
(D) one at a time

15) Which of the following has the biggest contribution to the final grade?

(A) each of the grade that students will get from class debates
(B) total grade that students will get from the five tests
(C) the grade that will be received from the reading assignments
(D) the grade that students will receive from their participation

Part 3

Read the conversation and answer questions 16 - 23

1   "Diana, darling. Why are you **fooling around** at home? Are you not supposed to study for your exams now?" asks Diana's mom.

"Mom, I am just having a break. I've been working all morning!", Diana responds.

"Working all morning! Doing what?" "I've just checked the school website and seen that
5   all your exams are this week, but you seem to be not studying but wasting your time doing nothing useful at home!", says mom angrily.

"Have you also checked my previous exam results? You'll see that all I get is A from all of them.", Diana says.

"Really? How come? I **barely** see you studying at home, what's more you say you don't
10   feel ready for exams. And in the end you get A's? How do you manage that?" asks her mom.

"I really feel nervous and **unconfident** before exams, mom. It's maybe because of not feeling sure of my knowledge", responds Diana.

"Alright, alright. Now tell me the secret key. How do you manage to get those good
15   marks then?", asks mom.

"Well, I guess I pay attention to my lessons a lot, I never get distracted by others during the lessons. I just focus on what the teacher tells. I take good notes. That's all I do. Oh, by the way. I stay after school to revise the subjects in the school library."

"I am really sorry for not trusting you, darling. I have always thought that you are behind
20   the class", states mom.

"No problem, mom. You have never seen me studying at home, but I study a lot at school. I don't need to study more", says Diana.

"So, tell me now. What have you been doing all morning? You said you had been working. What was it you were doing?", asks mom.

25   "You won't believe this, but I was cleaning up my bedroom and getting rid of the rubbish that you had been complaining about."

"I can't believe my eyes. That's my girl! Now I think you deserve a good prize. Tell me what you would like.", says mom.

"A car, mom." replies Diana. "That's funny." Her mom giggles.

16) What is Diana's mother complaining about?

(A) Diana's exam results
(B) Diana's laziness
(C) Diana's friends
(D) Her workload at home

17) We can infer from the first part of the conversation that _____ .

(A) Diana's mom is worried about the coming exams.
(B) Diana will fail the tests.
(C) Diana's mom is eager to help Diana with her studies.
(D) Diana is unsure about her success.

Part 3

18) In line 1, the phrase "fool around" can be best replaced by _____ .

(A) stroll around
(B) have trouble dealing with problems
(C) tease people around
(D) waste time doing nothing useful

19) In line 9, the word "barely" cannot be replaced by _____ .

(A) usually
(B) scarcely
(C) hardly
(D) almost never

20) In line 12, the word "unconfident" can be replaced by _____ .

(A) shocked
(B) unsure
(C) reliable
(D) disregard

21) According to the passage, all of the following statements are true about Diana EXCEPT FOR _____ .

(A) She pays attention in class.
(B) She never gets distracted during the lesson.
(C) She takes good notes.
(D) She studies at home.

22) According to the conversation what may be the reason of why Diana's mother thought that Diana was behind the class?

(A) She seems pretty preoccupied with her studying.
(B) She never sees her daughter studying.
(C) She doesn't listen to what her mother always tells her to do.
(D) She doesn't give enough importance to her mother's comments.

23) How may Diana's mother probably feel when she learns Diana has been doing the cleaning all morning?

(A) surprised
(B) undoubtful
(C) skeptical
(D) exhausted

Part 4

Read the conversation and answer questions 24 - 30

1   Some people believe that scientists should spend more time observing their pets rather than make investigations using expensive scientific equipment to predict natural disasters, especially earthquakes.
    Scientists don't seem to believe in the idea that animals possess a "sixth
5   sense",which enables them to have the natural ability to know or feel about things that occur or will occur before anybody else. However, the idea that animals tend to feel disasters; such as earthquakes, volcano eruptions and **others** is getting widely accepted by many people all around the world now. Although there is no concrete scientific proof to **validate** this hypothesis, it is interesting to study the animal
10 behaviors during or before a disaster.
    For instance, when humans can hear sounds in the range of 20 hertz to 20,000 kilohertz, certain animals, such as dogs, elephants, bats can go beyond this range when it comes to hearing.
    In the past, in China some farmers witnessed weird actions of their farm animals. The
15 Chinese scientists thought that the animals' running around in circles, and dogs' barking all night indicated a natural disaster. They decided that they could not risk people's lives and as a result, they decided to **evacuate** the city of Haichin, which was shortly afterwards hit by a huge earthquake. As a result of keeping people away from their houses, they were able to save lots of lives.
20 Many scientists now accept that the fact that animals can feel the forthcoming danger can't be pure coincidence. One explanation is that animal behavior may be linked to slight changes in the earth's magnetic field. Although human beings can't perceive such changes, animals are very sensitive to them. Therefore, their nervous system must be affected by these changes. Now scientists' duty is to discover exactly
25 which animals are affected in this way in order to be able to save more lives in the future.

24) What is mainly discussed about animal behaviors in the article?

(A) They have to be observed by scientists.
(B) They have a sixth sense that makes them feel disasters.
(C) They show weird actions at all times.
(D) Their reactions to new conditions are different from humanbeings'.

25) In line 7, the word "others" refers to _____ .

(A) natural disasters
(B) animals
(C) scientific equipment
(D) scientists

26) According to the text , all the following statements are true EXCEPT FOR _____ .

(A) Animals can feel forthcoming disasters.
(B) Animals are believed to have a sixth sense.
(C) Scientists use expensive equipment to predict disasters.
(D) The fact that animals have a natural way of feeling dangers is accepted by all scientists.

Part 4

27) In line 9, the word "validate" can be replaced by _____.

(A) dissuade
(B) affirm
(C) predict
(D) deny

28) According to the article, there _____.

(A) is no solid experimental clue that proves why animals sense danger.
(B) are not any scientists who study animal behavior.
(C) were times when scientists in China made some experiments on animals.
(D) were many animals saved during the earthquake in the city Haichin, China.

29) In line 17, the word "evacuate" is closest in meaning to _____

(A) empty
(B) load
(C) hold
(D) occupy

30) According to the text, all the following statements are wrong EXCEPT FOR _____

(A) Human beings can perceive magnetic field changes as well as animals.
(B) Animal behavior is on no account linked to huge magnetic field alterations.
(C) Scientists should find out which animals are affected by the magnetic field changes in order to save lives in the future.
(D) The fact that animals have a sense to feel disasters is just a coincidence.

Part 5

Read the text and answer questions 31 - 36.

1   Almost everyone knows what social media is. Even the people in the most remote parts of the world may have heard of Facebook and Twitter. In today's world, we cannot imagine a world without social media, but in the past, not even long ago we didn't have any chance to connect to the internet.

5   The first social media site was the website called Six Degrees. SixDegrees.com lasted from 1997 to 2001. It started after the six degrees of separation concept which means any person on the planet can be connected to any other person through a chain of acquaintances. Six Degrees allowed users to create a profile and then find other users.

10 By the end of the second millennium, over 100 million people had access to the internet. People began to utilize chat rooms and other social sites to make friends, date or discuss topics in the forum sites. In 2003 the website MySpace was popular to set up a profile and make friends. This inspired websites like Facebook.

15 Apart from Facebook, another website LinkedIn started to be used by millions of people. In fact, most of the social media websites today are similar to this. They all have some kind of unique quality. While MySpace was a general social media site, LinkedIn was, or is, for professional use of business related people to connect
20 with each other to find jobs and socialized and for other business reasons.

31) What is the first paragraph mainly about?

(A) how social media improved
(B) Facebook users
(C) social media users' lives
(D) MySpace users

32) "Even the people in the most remote parts of the world may have heard of Facebook and Twitter" with this statement, we can conclude that _____ .

(A) People use Facebook more than Twitter.
(B) Facebook and Twitter are worldwide popular.
(C) Almost no one has heard of Facebook and Twitter.
(D) There is no connection to the internet in remote countries.

33) In line 3, the phrase not even long ago implies that _____ .

(A) Access to the internet started a long time before social media.
(B) Social media use is not recent.
(C) Internet access has come to our world recently.
(D) Social media use started a long time ago.

34) According to the passage, which of the following is not true about the website called Six Degrees?

(A) It lasted for six years.
(B) Anyone on the planet can connect to any other person.
(C) It was the first social media site.
(D) It started in the last years of 20th century.

Part 5

35) In line 11, the word <u>utilize</u> probably means _____ .

(A) discuss
(B) make use of
(C) connect to
(D) supply

36) What makes LinkedIn different from other social websites?

(A) It is for professional use.
(B) They all have unique qualities.
(C) People use LinkedIn just for making friends.
(D) People don't prefer LinkedIn much.

Part 6

Read the passage and answer questions 37 - 42.

1   Agatha Christie, born with the name Agatha Mary Clarissa Miller was and still is the most-selling author of all times. She was a mystery writer. She is known for her detective novels and short story collections. Her books have sold millions of copies and have been translated into more than 100 languages. She was also a well-known playwright.

5   Born in 1890 in Devon, England, she died in 1976 in Wallington, Oxfordshire. She didn't have a proper school education. Instead, she was educated by her mother at home. Her career as a writer took off when she was working as a nurse during World War I. She wrote her first novel "The Mysterious Affair at Styles" and created the character Poirot, who was an eccentric and egoistic Belgian detective. She used this character in her 25 novels.

10   Christie's play "The Mousetrap" set a world record as it was run at one theatre for more than 20 years with 8,862 performances. Most of her plays and novels were adapted into films and her other works were also adapted for television. One of her most notable film adaptations includes "The Murder on the Orient Express" and "Witness for the Prosecution" was adapted into a successful film.

15   In 1928 Agatha Christie divorced her husband as he had an affair with another woman. Then in 1930 she married an archaeology professor Max Mallowan. She attended several of his expeditions and later in 1946 she wrote the **memoir** "Come, Tell Me How You Live", which was a historical account of her trips. During those years she wrote "Murder at the Vicarage", which became another classic.

20   Her characters in her novels became as popular as her fame with her stories. Most popular ones, Poirot and Marple are her well-known detectives. She used these characters in dozens of her novels and short stories. Other notable Christie characters were Tuppence and Tommy Beresford, Colonel Race, Parker Pyne and Ariadne Oliver.

   In 1974, she made her last public appearance for the opening night of the play "Murder on
25   Orient Express" and died two years later.

37) What can be the best title for this text?

(A) Agatha's Best-Selling Novels
(B) Educated at Home
(C) Agatha Christie's marriage life
(D) The Queen of Mystery

38) Which of the statement is true about Agatha?

(A) Agatha lived a solitary life.
(B) Agatha wrote only long novels.
(C) Agatha used the character, named Poirot in many of her novels.
(D) Agatha Mary Clarissa Miller was the false name that she used.

Part 6

39) According to the text, the following statements are true EXCEPT _____

(A) Agatha Christie was educated by her mom at home.
(B) She wrote novels, short stories, plays that became popular worldwide.
(C) Christie died at the age of 86.
(D) "The Murder on the Orient Express" was her first book.

40) Referring to the text, which of the following is *not correct*?

(A) "The Mousetrap" set a world record.
(B) "The Mysterious Affair at Styles" was about an archaeology professor.
(C) "Come, Tell Me How You Live" was a memoir.
(D) "Witness for the Prosecution" was adapted into a film.

41) In line 17, what does the word "*memoir*" mean?

(A) historical account
(B) memorial
(C) article
(D) essay

42) Which of the following is *not* one of Christie's characters?

(A) Colonel Race
(B) Tuppence
(C) Max Mallowan
(D) Tommy Beresford

Section 3
LISTENING SCRIPTS

Practice Test 1

Part 1 (Questions 1 - 10)

1) **(Principal):** I'd like to inform all of you about the Spring Program that will last for 7 days commencing from April 2nd. To enroll the program, you must complete and submit the registration forms that will be sent to your email address today. Programs will be between 8 am. and 3 pm. . Breakfast will be provided, but you will have to bring your packed lunch with you. The attendants should use their own way of transportation to school. For further information don't hesitate to contact Mr.Bennet, the program organiser.

2) **(Principal):** Attention please. I have a really important announcement to make. According to the decision given by the school board, there will be elections to choose student leaders from each class level, these elections will be held next month. So, if you think that you have a capability of inspiring and leading others, you can be a candidate or you can nominate a student for this duty. We request from the board to get the candidate names, announcing the nominees and arrange the exact date for the elections. That's all for now.

3) **(Teacher):** Now, class. As you know we have covered all the units from our course book so far, there will be a revision quiz for you to do some time next week in order to see how much you have understood the grammatical patterns and vocabulary items we have completed up to now. I want you to revise the subjects by doing the progress check questions that are at the end of the workbook. This quiz is very important, because it will give you a chance to see how much you have understood the topics so far. Remember that at the end of next month you will be taking the final exams. So good luck. Any questions?

4) **(Scientist):** Hi everyone. My name is John Miller. I am here today to inform you about the latest studies we have been carrying out with our doctorate students on the effects of VR, which is called Virtual Reality. I know this subject will get your attention, because it is a common concern of many people in today's world. However, things are not always as they seem. Our studies show that the negative effects of using this technology outweigh the positive impact on humans.So, I'll start with…………

5) **(Principal):** I have an announcement to make. Our school counsellor Mrs. Watson has retired on age grounds. We are here to introduce to you Mr. Bringley as our new counsellor. He will arrange new programs with you, and assist you to overcome your learning problems by means of individual study schedules. So he is here to monitor each of your successes and help you overcome your individual problems. He is going to plan your educational learning process and will help you whenever you have problems on any subjects. So you can easily reach him whenever you need help in every kind of issues.

Part 1 (Questions 1 - 10)

6) **(Principal):** As a parent your participation in your children's education is of great value to their achievement in school. We are here to inform you about all the facilities and opportunities provided at our school and we would like to let you learn about our school procedures and requirements.So if you are willing to contribute to your child's school success, we would be happy to see you attend the workshops that will last for three weeks starting on 14th May. You will find the details of the workshops in the leaflet given to you.

7) **(Teacher):** Because of many reasons, some living things become extinct. There are two types of extinction; the ones that are caused by consequences of natural events and the ones that are triggered by human activities. Climate changes that result in severe weather conditions with long seasons, sudden ups and downs in temperature, changing sea levels, tsunamis, lanslides, cosmic radiation andacid rains are all natural causes. Human beings also play a big role on extinction. The more humans damage nature, the more disasters happen and as a result some species cannot survive.

8) **(Doctor):** You may feel a sudden discomfort, or heaviness in your chest. Or, you may have difficulty breathing. If so, these symptoms may be followed by dizziness and weakness.You may start to sweat a lot during these symptoms. You can mistakenly think that it is caused by indigestion or heartburn. You must consult a doctor in this case, because these symptoms show that you may be in a more serious health condition. Have you heard of "coronary artery disease"? It is a congestive heart failure or heart attack, which is a serious case that should be checked by a doctor immediately.

9) **(Expert):** Some scientific statistics indicate that more than 8 million hectares of forests are lost all around the world each year. The world is facing a big problem of deforestation. So far, it is estimated that half of the world's forests have been destructed, which means our universe loses over 20 million acres of forests each year. Today our main concern is to talk about reasons that cause this huge loss of forests. There are several reasons for this loss. One and the most important one is urbanization, which means cutting down trees to clear the land to be used for housing. Harvesting timber to make furniture and homes is another reason. We can say …….

10) **(Consultant):** I know it's hard for you to concentrate on studying while there are many distracting things around you. If you want a better lifestyle, a better career in the future, you must gain some useful habits. The more systematically and consistently you study, the better results you get. If you want better grades, all you need is to have more effective study habits. The key to effective studying isn't cramming or studying longer, but studying smarter. First of all, try to think positively while studying. Avoid having negative thoughts like "I am such a mess, I'll never succeed."! Don't compare yourself with others! Just remind yourself of your skills and capabilities. It is that simple!

Part 2 (Questions 11 - 15)

(Boy): Mrs. Wellsh, do you have some time, please?

(Mrs. Wellsh): Yes, of course. Brian. What's the problem?

(Boy): You know, we're supposed to hand in an essay on "technological innovations" next Monday.

(Mrs. Wellsh): You sound as if you haven't even started it yet. Am I right?

(Boy): Not exactly, ma'am. I was just going to ask you for an extension on it?

(Mrs. Wellsh): Why do you need an extension? I gave all of you enough time to complete this in 3 weeks. I think this is quite a reasonable period for such an assignment.

(Boy): Yes, you are right. Well, I haven't had enough time to do the necessary research on the subject.
As a result, I haven't finished it. You know, I haven't been able to attend classes for weeks.

(Mrs. Wellsh): Why couldn't you attend classes?

(Boy): I've been out of town, you know basketball tournaments started a few weeks ago.

(Mrs. Wellsh): What is your priority Brian? You must get your priorities straight. Don't you want to be a graduate?

(Boy): Of course, that's why I am here. I must finish college and get a good job later on.

(Mrs. Wellsh): So, you should be aware of what you have to do. You're supposed to focus on your studies and spare your leisure time for your hobbies.

(Boy): To be honest, I must attend all the games, I can't risk my sports scholarship. In order to complete my education years successfully, I need to be a successful sports person, too.

(Mrs. Wellsh): Now that you are being frank with me, I can make an exception, but this is just for you.

(Boy): I do appreciate this and promise that I'll be very successful in your lesson, ma'am.

(Mrs. Wellsh): I hope this will not happen again. I won't accept another request, Brian.

(Boy): I promise, I will always hand in my assignments on time.

(Mrs. Wellsh): I do hope so.

Part 3 (Questions 16 - 21)

(James): Hey, Jane. Did you watch our match the other day?

(Jane): Of course, I did James. Congratulations on winning. Your team's performance was unbelievable.
My friends and I were impressed with how well each of you on the team played.

(James): Especially Steward. He did a great job, didn't he?

(Jane): He's an outstanding goalkeeper. He made quite a lot of good saves. You played so well as a striker, too.

(James): I can't deny it! I guess I did well.

(Jane): Of course you did. You scored three goals. When is the next game?

(James): Not this week. We have three matches two weeks later and two more the following weeks. Are you gonna come watch us again?

(Jane): I'll do my best to make it. How is school going, by the way?

(James): My lesson load has doubled at school.

(Jane): How come! You are only in the foundation year, aren't you?

(James): Yes, I am. But I am doing a double major.

(Jane): Isn't it hard for you?

(James): It is but I enjoy it. You know, killing two birds with one stone! When I graduate I will have two degrees that means I will have more opportunities for my future career life.

(Jane): I guess you are doing the best thing. Does playing in the school team contribute anything to your education life?

(James): Yes, it does. How do you think I could finance my studies? Education fees, the cost of accommodation and other expenses are really high, you know.

(Jane): My dad says if I cannot finish school this year, I will have to look for a part-time job to support my education costs.

(James): Do you think he is right?

(Jane): Yeah, I guess he is. However, to be frank, I am not into working!

(James): Come on, Jane!

Part 4 (Questions 22 - 26)

(Father): Lucy, what is all this mess?

(Girl): It is not a mess, dad.

(Father): You don't call this a mess? The room is covered with sheets of paper torn and thrown around everywhere!

(Girl): I am working on something important!

(Father): Can you tell me what it is?

(Girl): Yesterday I saw an ad on the school bulletin board for a free writing contest.

(Father): I didn't know you were good at writing! What are you gonna write?

(Girl): I am trying to write a short story. You know how much I love fancy stories with supernatural characters, fairies, trolls. I have so much in my mind but I cannot concentrate.

(Father): Because there are so many things to distract your attention in this room.

(Girl): Come on dad!

(Father): Your mobile phone keeps ringing, you are always online, there is non-stop disturbance from your friends with their mails or their texts! Not to mention instagram messages!

(Girl): I can't reject my friends' calls, can I? I am not always online. My laptop is on, but I am just sitting on my bed trying to focus on my writing.

(Father): OK darling, I give in. I know it's not worth wasting my voice, because my warnings will not be heard. You and your friends are web addicts!

(Girl): That's not true! We are just using the social network a bit more frequently than adults. Of course, not all the time.

(Father): If only you would spend more time on reading books than wasting your time on the net!

(Girl): All my friends are like this.

Part 4 (Questions 22 - 26)

(Father): I know all the parents complain about the same issue, I think. It's no use talking about it over and over. Now, tell me about the prize.

(Girl): Oh, the best part of this contest is that there are cash prizes.

(Father): What is your plan with the money you will get?

(Girl): You sound as if I am going to win the prize.

(Father): I trust you, darling. But you should turn off your laptop, don't use your phone and sit at your desk and concentrate on your work.

(Girl): Alright, dad.

(Father): When is it due?

(Girl): I have two weeks to send my writing.

(Father): Good luck! Oh, by the way clean up the mess here.

(Girl): (She puffs) Alright dad!

Part 5 (Questions 27 - 30)

(Biologist): Honey bees use their senses to find the best flowers so that they can find the best pollen and nectar to make honey. While trying to find the best flower, they use smell, color, shape, location, petal textures and time of day. When they have found the best quality flower, they suck the nectar from the flower, they store it in their special honey stomach.

When honey bees have discovered where the best flowers are, they use special ways to tell the others what they have found. Bees have a special kind of language; they communicate by means of dancing. The worker bees are called honey bee workers. They produce honey. These bees communicate by performing a series of movements, which often referred to as the "waggle dance", to show other workers where food sources are. Scout bees fly from the colony in search of pollen and nectar. Every morning, worker bees set off to find food. When they find some, they return home to let the other bees know where it is. They do this by performing different dances. If the worker bees find food nearby, they do one type of dance. The type of dance also shows which way the bees should fly to find the food. And the length of the dance shows how far it is. A short dance shows there isn't far to go. The speed of the dance also tells important information; dancing extremely fast means there is a lot of food.

Part 6 (Questions 31 - 36)

(Historian): Today we are going to talk about the two old different civilizations; Mesopotamia and Egypt. There were some similarities between them. First of all, if we take a look at the constructions they built, we notice how they look a bit like each other with minor differences. The Egyptians built pyramids and Mesopotamians built ziggurats, about which we know very little. Pyramids are a lot more well-known. Both Egyptians and Mesopotamians built large structures. The Egyptians built pyramids in large areas, many of which are still standing. The Mesopotamians also built these pyramid-shaped constructions in large areas, too. If we mention about the differences, the main difference is that their shapes and sizes are not completely the same. The Egyptian pyramid is more triangular. The sides of a pyramid are smooth and rather steep. On the other hand, the ziggurats have steps on the sides. They look as if the constructions are built by putting boxes in different sizes on top of one another. There are stairs to the top on the sides of a ziggurat. On the other hand, there are no stairs on the pyramids. Do you know why they had these stairs? There existed temples at the top of a ziggurat. So the Mesopotamians climbed the stairs to reach their temple. This also shows us another difference. The Mesopotamian priests used ziggurats to worship their gods. However, pyramids are not temples, they are tombs for the pharaohs, the kings of ancient Egypt. Many pharaohs had pyramids built to be their tombs when they died.

Part 7 (Questions 37 - 42)

(Teacher): The world's most accurate radio telescope is in Green Bank, West Virginia, in the USA. It is called "Green Bank Telescope". It was built by NRAO. It is called "The National Radio Astronomy Observatory". It welcomes scientists from all around the world every year, regardless of which country they are from. Scientists have been using this telescope especially to search for comets, black holes and stars. More than 1000 scientists have used this telescope in the last decade, because it is the best of its kind in the world. NRAO also organizes programs in education useful for teachers, students and the general public.

There are some special rules in the town where the telescope is located. For example; wi-fi is banned, the area around the telescope is a quiet zone. For this reason, the residents are not allowed to use cellphones. Cellphones and other devices that can connect to the internet are illegal. About 140 local people live in the town without using any wireless technology. The reason for this is that any kind of signal may interfere with the telescope's work. That's why, about 13,000 square mile area is known as a National Quiet Zone.

In order to detect the area and to see if there is someone violating the law, there is a surveillance truck that patrols in and around the town acting as a "radio police". The truck monitors radio frequencies and checks the area to keep it under control.

Paractice Test 2

Part 1 (Questions 1 - 10)

1) **(Biology teacher):** There are many deadly animals that are man-eaters. The deadliest ones are sharks and big cats. These animals are capable killers. Other dangerous animals like crocodiles and alligators also eat human flesh. Sometimes they don't need to be provoked to attack people. It is always considered that only these kinds of animals eat human flesh. However, there are some humans that are man-eaters. Some tribes along the Amazon River who lead a primitive life still remain cannibals. Besides, ...

2) **(Teacher):** Once upon a time, there was a girl named Becky. She was curious, wise and sensitive. Even though she was the youngest, each member of the family looked up to her. They thought she knew the answers to everything. She had a special status among her relatives, because she had been taught to be kind and respectful to others. She would read a lot and always wanted to learn new things. She was always open to new ideas. She was broad-minded. Her parents had always told her to stick up for her family, because "family" meant everything in Becky's home.

3) **(Science teacher):** As most of you know, light moves incredibly fast. To be more exact, it moves about 300.000 meters per second. That's known as the speed of light. As far as we know, it's impossible to exceed the speed of light. Measurements of the speed of light have always been a challenging motivation that has encouraged scientists for centuries. It has been considered that speed is infinite. This assumption was dispelled by the Danish astronomer Ole Romer in 1676.

4) **(History teacher):** The New World has always been thought to be discovered by Cristopher Columbus. Do you get what I mean by saying the New World? Yes, James. You answer. Yeah, you are right. That's America. Well, Christopher Columbus wasn't the first explorer to reach and discover both North and South America. The Vikings reached some parts of Canada by around the year 1000. Besides the Vikings, it has been proven that the Romans arrived in the New World centuries earlier before them. There are still other beliefs and rumors as well. Now let me talk about the ....

5) **(Teacher):** I'd like to make an announcement to students who would like to take part in the Spelling Bee Competition. I have just hung a form on the students' bulletin board so that anyone interested in taking part in this competition can write their names down. Write your class number under your name as well. The competition will take place in the school hall next Friday at 4 pm. For further questions, you can contact Mr. Dean at any time during school hours.

Part 1 (Questions 1 - 10)

6) **(Teacher):** As you all know, technology has improved a lot and each day we can see new innovations that amaze all of us. I want to talk about a new invention today, but before starting I'd like to ask you a question. What happens when you drop your mobile phone, which is worth hundreds of dollars? These phones are so fragile that once you drop you can damage its screen or it may become useless. Engineers have found a solution for this. They have created a transparent flexible screen that helps bendable phones. This flexible screen allows a mobile phone to bend and stretch, which makes it durable. That is to say, you can't easily break or damage your phone. For example, you could flex the phone forwards or backwards.

7) **(Teacher):** Now, class I want you to talk about an interesting activity you have tried. Who wants to volunteer to speak first? Oh, David ... Let's start with you.

   (David): I'd like to talk about an activity I tried the other day. I am sure most of you haven't even heard about its name. This is a very nice outdoor activity called land-yatching. They also call it beach-yatching and land-sailing. There is a little chariot with three wheels and a big sail. You sit on the chariot and catch the wind in the sail to make the chariot move. You do not have to do it on a beach. Any flat land will do.

8) **(Teacher):** In this lesson, you'll learn what makes a piece of writing narrative. Do you remember the children story "The story of the three billy goats"? It is a very good example of narrative writing, as it tells us a story. This kind of writing is categorized as fiction, because it is based on imaginative events or stories that didn't really happen. However, some nonfiction can also involve a story. Also biographies and autobiographies have stories, too. That means we write about stories in a narrative style. In short, whether it is fiction or nonfiction, biography or autobiography, when we tell a story of an event or a story of someone's life, we use narrative writing styles. All stories must have characters, a plot and a setting in a narrative writing.

9) **(Lecturer):** The concept of "Smoking is unhealthy" is widely accepted all over the world. However, even though people are aware of its harm, they cannot quit this habit. In order to encourage people to stop smoking, governments should legislate new laws to protect their citizens. Smoking is banned in most public places and closed areas. However, there are still special smoking places. The more you restrict people from doing something, the more they desire to do it.

10) **(Lecturer):** When certain gases in Earth's atmosphere trap heat, warming starts. These gases keep heat from escaping. It is like the glass walls of a greenhouse. That's why, we call this the Greenhouse Effect. When sunrise shines onto the Earth's surface, it's absorbed and radiated back into the atmosphere. There, some of the heat is trapped by "greenhouse" gases. If there are more greenhouse gases in the atmosphere, there is more heat getting trapped there.

Part 2 (Questions 11 - 17)

(Bill): Hi, Fiona. Did you hear about the singing competition that is organized by our school?

(Fiona): No, did they announce it in the school magazine or on the school website? I always check them, but I haven't seen or heard about such an event.

(Bill): No, the ad was on the school bulletin board. The moment I read it, I thought to myself that you should enter.

(Fiona): I am not sure if I'm good enough. I can't really sing rap or hip hop, you know. And I am not in favor of singing opera, either. What kind of music is required?

(Bill): None of them. Don't worry. This is a pop music contest.

(Fiona): Sounds good to me. Can you tell me when it will be held, Bill? I hope it's not on the weekend, you know, my basketball coach will be mad if I miss even one practice! I wouldn't risk my sports scholarship.

(Bill): Come on, you have nothing on Sundays. The competition is on Sunday. It starts at 11 am and it lasts about 3 hours.

(Fiona): Does the competition take place at the auditorium or the music room?

(Bill): Neither. It's at the Trinity Leisure Center.

(Fiona): Oh, there will be a big audience. I might be too nervous.

(Bill): Don't be! You should be confident. You've got a brilliant voice.

(Fiona): Thanks, Bill. I need to check it out myself. Then I'll think it over. I have to ask my parents as well. Oh, by the way where is the advertisement?

(Bill): It's on the bulletin board which is in Hall A, the second floor. You will see it next to the Students' Affairs Office.

(Fiona): Thanks, we'll talk later. Bye for now.

(Bill): I hope you'll join it. Bye.

Part 3 (Questions 18 - 24)

(Diana): How are you getting on with your Science assignment, David?

(David): I finished it the other day. I have other assignments to be completed soon.

(Diana): Who are you working with on the English literature assignment?

(David): Most probably with Tom. Jennifer and Tim are working together, so I suppose Tom wouldn't mind working with me. Besides, he's really good at literature. And you are Ryan's partner, aren't you Diana?

(Diana): That's right, but Ryan hates literature. I think I will be the one who will do most of the work!

(David): When are you going to meet up?

(Diana): We're supposed to meet up after school on Friday at his place to get started, but you know he keeps changing his mind. He never sticks to his plans.

(David): Yeah, I know. At least you have arranged to meet. I haven't been able to reach Tom for days. Has he been away?

(Diana): I guess he's skipping school. You can find him at Brain's cafe, he is a regular. It's his favorite place.

(David): I just wonder whether we will be able to finish it on time.

(Diana): Don't worry. We have two more weeks to hand in all the assignments.

(David): You think it's enough?

(Diana): Yeap, I'll help you with your part. But first of all, try to do your best to reach Tom and decide on the topic of your assignment, then the rest will go smoothly.

(David): I guess you are right. I shouldn't worry too much. I can complete everything. Do you have the list of the essay topics for the literature assignment?

(Diana): Yes, I do. Mrs. Abbott has sent the list to all of us. Haven't you received it?

(David): My computer is broken. I can't check my mail. I think I should use the computer in the school library.

(Diana): Good idea.

Part 4 (Questions 25 - 30)

(Teacher): Good morning everyone. I just want to talk to you about our trip to Crater Lake. Have you all received my e-mail?

(Jonathan): Yes, madam but I think there are some points that are missing in the mail.

(Teacher): Like what, Jonathan?

(Jonathan): I think you only attached the first page of the information leaflet, because there is no information about when or how we are going to get there!

(Teacher): Oh, let me tell you all about the program then. We are going to travel by coach. It will pick us up on Tuesday at 5 pm.

(George): Where is the meeting point?

(Teacher): I want you to be here in front of the school gate by half past 4 pm at the latest. Don't make us wait for you. The trip will take 6 hours, so you will be tired when we get there. We'll check-in the hotel as soon as we get there. We'll stay at a lovely lodge, called The Cratle Lodge. The following morning, we'll be taken on the Wizard Islander's boat cruise. You'll be amazed to see the calm blue water of the lake.

(Peter): What do we have to bring with us?

(Teacher): Your summer clothes, but don't forget to bring warm clothes as well, because it may be cold in the evenings. Oh, by the way we'll have a chance to do scuba-diving. Don't forget your scuba diving equipment. The lake happens to be the deepest lake in the U.S. and the ninth deepest in the world. There's plenty to explore in the crystal-clear shallows; such as lava formations, wildlife, moss meadows. Is there anyone who doesn't know how to swim?

(Peter): I think only Lucy, but she is not here today.
In fact, she isn't coming to the trip. She couldn't get permission from her parents.

(Teacher): Alright then, I think everything is clear enough. Isn't it?

(Berry): What are we going to do with the form you sent us?

(Teacher): Thanks for reminding me about that Berry. Bring in the forms filled and signed by your parents tomorrow. Now, guys that's all for now. Hurry up to your classes immediately.

Part 5 (Questions 31 - 35)

(George): Are you going to attend the conference tomorrow?

(Mary): Which conference?

(George): Haven't you heard of it? Mr. Abegail is going to tell us all about the MUN and how to participate in the committees

(Mary): I don't know what you are talking about. What is this MUN?

(George): Let me explain. MUN is short form of Model United Nations. It is an academic activity where students can learn about diplomacy, international relations, and the United Nations with its principles.

(Mary): Do you mean you join lectures to learn about diplomacy?

(George): Of course not, there are no lectures. Students assume the role of representatives of different countries they choose. We call them delegates. Before the conferences, all the delegates search and learn about the geological, social and political values and issues of the country they are going to represent.

(Mary): What then?

(George): Then participants show their negotiating and oratory skills while representing their countries. They talk about the problems of the countries and suggest solutions.

(Mary): What is the aim of these activities?

(George): The aim of MUN differs from conference to conference, but usually it is supposed to educate participating students about the workings of an international organization such as the UN. These conferences broaden the view and knowledge of the students about what is going on around the world, they become more aware of the problems that countries face.

(Mary): This is so meaningful. What age groups can attend these conferences?

(George): Oh, it depends. A Model United Nations is a simulation of different UN organs for high school or university students. Today there are small conferences of secondary school students too.

(Mary): When was MUN established?

(George): As far as I know, the oldest modern simulation is the Harvard United Nations, established in 1951. The oldest MUN in Europe started with the The Hague International Model.

Part 6 (Questions 36 - 42)

(Teacher): I'm sure all of you have heard about Edgar Allan Poe. Today we're going to talk about his life and his works. Poe was born in 1809 and died in 1849. His short life was quite miserable. He lost his parents when he was only three years old and was brought up by a foster family. He faced many problems all his life. He was addicted to gambling and he had drinking problems, too. He suffered from a serious depression. The dark side of his life had a great impact on his writing. He was one of the greatest writers who contributed a lot to the world of literature. He created a new vision by writing horror. He also wrote some early science fiction and detective stories. He is considered to be one of the founders of the modern short story. He is most famous for his horror stories, of course. The most well-known ones are "The Fall of the House of Usher", "The Masque of the Red Death" and "The Pit and the Pendulum". Each story deals with death. This is his main topic in his stories. His poems were also popular. His works of art are still read and loved by millions of people around the World.

Paractice Test 3

Part 1 (Questions 1 - 10)

1) **(Math teacher):** Today we are going to study the history of "Pi". As you know, Pi is the name given to the ratio of the circumference of a circle, which means the distance around the circle by the diameter. How big or small a circle is doesn't make any difference. Pi always stays the same. Ancient civilizations considered that there was a fixed ratio of circumference to diameter which was equal to number three. Archimedes was credited as the first person to calculate Pi theoretically. In 1761 Lambert proved Pi was irrational. In 1882 Lindeman proved that Pi was transcendental. Mathematicians of today are still working on "Pi".

2) **(Teacher):** It was a cold, snowy winter afternoon. John and Mary went out to make a snowman. They made a huge one. Then they called out for their parents to show what they had done. The father liked the snowman so much and asked the kids; "Do you know when the snowman melts it leaves us a gift that lasts all year? What do you think it is?". The kids thought for a while, but couldn't find the answer. The father explained; "When spring comes, the snowman starts to melt. As it melts, the melting crystals turn into ice and then become water. The water goes deep into the ground. Then water causes the soil to get ready to grow flowers, vegetables and fruit. So kids, do you understand what the gift is?

3) **(Class teacher):** I want to announce that the school authority and the teachers have decided to dedicate Mondays as "Help a Friend Day". We believe that if you help one person at least once a week, you will understand how valuable supporting someone is. Friendships grow as much as you encourage each other. So we'd like to get your suggestions as well. The main reason why I am making this announcement is to get your ideas on what could be done on that day and ask you to write your suggestions on a piece of paper. Your suggestions will be collected in this box and then they will be evaluated by the school authority. Any questions?

4) **(Principal):** Today we are very proud to announce that one of our students in Year 8, named Roxanne Guilford has been nominated to represent our school in the Annual Secondary Schools Mental Maths Competitions. As she was unanimously elected with your votes, we believe that she is going to display an excellent performance. We would like to see your support by attending the competitions.

5) **(Principal):** Unfortunately due to the inclement weather conditions, the school will be closed today and tomorrow. According to the weather forecast, there will be severe thunderstorms with heavy rain all the way up the East Coast. For this reason, the former Year 12 Certificate Collection Evening has been postponed until Friday at 5 pm. If the weather doesn't get better, we will consider another date for the Certificate Collection. In that case, the school secretary will text you about the date and time.

Part 1 (Questions 1 - 10)

6) **(Teacher):** Congratulations, Tilda. You got the highest mark in the class on your report.

   (Tilda): Thank you. I really worked hard on it.

   (Teacher): You sure did. Have you ever considered writing for the school paper? Your writing is excellent and your choice of vocabulary in your essays is great. You are such a gifted writer.

   (Tilda): Thank you. Although I haven't thought about it until this moment, I think it will be a wonderful experience for me.

   (Teacher): I am sure, it will. I also think that this experience will make your writing better. Talk to the person in charge of it and get started right away.

7) **(Teacher):** Jane, I think you should get involved in our project "Animals in Danger". I've seen you working hard on campaigns and activities for endangered animals.

   (Jane): I'd love to, but my mother thinks I am wasting too much time on such projects. She thinks these projects distract my attention. She says I should focus on my studies more.

   (Teacher): Oh, come on. Projects are part of our lessons. I'd better get in touch with her.

8) **(Girl):** What John did during the exam of Mr. Harvey's lesson was unacceptable. To me, he should have been more careful while choosing his words when he was talking to the teacher. He was rude, disrespectful and what he did was wrong. He talked to the teacher as if it was not his own fault but the teacher's. He cheated in the exam and denied it. Even though Mr. Harvey saw him cheating, he said the teacher was blaming him for nothing in a really impolite way. I think John doesn't deserve to be in this school. This is not the only case, everybody is fed up with his mischievious behavior. The school authority must do something about his misbehavior!

9) **(Head Teacher):** Now, I'd like to give you some information about the bike ride that will be held during the second week of May. The participants will cycle a total of 25 kilometres. There will be five stops along the way so that the cyclists can rest a bit. If there are more than 30 participants, there will be another ride the following day. What you will need is your helmet and bike. You can wear shorts and a T-shirt. You don't need to wear a track suit. By the way, the ride will start outside the school at 9:30.

10) **(Counsellor):** As I was checking your grades you received very low marks in chemistry. If you can get some bonus points, you can pull off a B or even an A. All you need to do is to get extra-credit projects involving some work in the lab. I suggest that you think of an experiment that you'd like to do. You could get some chemistry books in the library to get some ideas. But check with your teacher for approval before you start the project. If your teacher doesn't consent to it, there's no use to begin.

Part 2 (Questions 11 - 16)

(Brian): Jennifer, after school we are thinking of going to the new mall, the one that opened on High Street. Would you like to join us?

(Jennifer): No, I am afraid I can't. My sister is coming from England this afternoon.

(Brian): Was she on vacation in England?

(Jennifer): No, she was in England for education.

(Brian): What is she studying there?

(Jennifer): Her major is music. She is at the Royal Academy of Music.

(Brian): Wow, so cool!

(Jennifer): Yeap, it is one of the best universities in the World.

(Brian): What about her future plans?

(Jennifer): She wants to improve her music skills and she is thinking of doing her masters there. And guess what? She is even considering living in England afterwards. Who knows?

(Brian): I wish her all the best. So, are you going to spend your whole day with her?

(Jennifer): I'll pick her up from the airport, then we'll visit our grandparents. They haven't seen her for months.

(Brian): That means, you'll be busy all day! Next time, then.

(Jennifer): How about tomorrow? Why don't you all come to my house? It would be nice for my sister as well. Remember the last time we were talking about universities abroad, you said that you had always wanted to study in a European country. If you come tomorrow, you can ask my sister anything you want to learn about university life in the UK.

(Brian): That'll be great. I have so many questions. Even though I want to study abroad, I still wonder whether I can cope with the different culture and the new living conditions of a foreign country. What kind of difficulties would I face? How we live in America is quite different from the lifestyle in Europe.

(Jennifer): Most Europeans think that everything is huge in America. They have more conventional and less luxurious lifestyles in Europe. The houses are smaller than ours. It may be weird to adopt to a new life, but then you'll get used to it. My sister loves it. Of course, she had difficult times in the beginning. But now you see, she wants to continue her future life there. She doesn't mind settling in the UK.

(Brian): I guess, I will have to talk to her. OK, I'll drop by tomorrow. See you then.

(Jennifer): Take care for now. Bye.

Part 3 (Questions 17 - 22)

(James): Why did Mr. Black want to see you in his office, Donna?

(Donna): Oh, for that science fair.

(James): What science fair? I've never heard about it.

(Donna): There will be a fair in April. It is an organisation held by the school board. This year will be the first year of the organisation and the school is thinking about holding it every year in April. They have already invited 10 schools for the fair.

(James): That's something we don't know! How come you learn such things before us!

(Donna): Because I have been working in the science lab on an experiment with Mr. Black, so I learn everything.

(James): Are you the only student who will be involved in the fair?

(Donna): I am really not sure about that, because there will be more than one competition. There will be two kinds of competitions, one of which will include ten groups of 3 students and the other will have individual participants.

(James): What do you mean by that?

(Donna): I mean participants will compete individually. There will be only one student from each participating school.

(James): In which group will you participate?

(Donna): I will be on my own, because I have been working on an experiment for so long and Mr. Black thinks that my work is so valuable. He says it is so good that it has a chance to get the biggest prize.

(James): There's one thing that bothers me. Why didn't Mr. Black tell us anything about this fair?

(Donna): As far as I know, the students to take part in this fair are picked in accordance with the projects they have been working on. Teachers choose three projects that they like the most and then they present these to the commission that consists of one science teacher from each school. Next, the commission decides on who will take part in the competitions during the fair.

(James): Wow, you must have done something really good then. I have to congratulate you on that and wish you good luck.

(Donna): Thank you.

Part 4 (Questions 23 - 28)

(Susan): I am so overloaded with exams and assignments. I really don't know how to handle them.

(Robert): I understand. Teachers seem to be pushing us very hard these days. I'm totally occupied with loads of tasks waiting to be completed, too.

(Susan): Can you do any extracurricular activities?

(Robert): Are you kidding me! My parents would never let me do anything, but study! They don't even let me play basketball on the weekends. They just want me to focus on my studies.

(Susan): Don't you think it would be relaxing and motivating to take up a new hobby or sport?

(Robert): That would be great! I wish my parents would reconsider this, but they won't. Well, what about you? Are you doing anything interesting these days? Forget about school and lessons.

(Susan): I am writing articles for the school newspaper, besides I am also working on the school yearbook committee.

(Robert): Wow, that's a lot! That's why you feel so busy. Which of these activities keep you the most occupied?

(Susan): Writing for the newspaper is not that difficult for me. I should write one article for each week. So it takes me two or three hours a week, for which I spare my weekend. But the school yearbook work is hard. The committee members gather at least twice or three times a week after school and we talk about what to include or exclude in the book. We revise students' writings and so on. It keeps us very busy.

(Robert): Good luck with all that. Your schedule is really packed. You should take a break.

(Susan): I guess, you're right.

Part 5 (Questions 29 - 33)

(Head teacher): I'd like to welcome Professor Alice Wolfard, an important gemologist. She is here today to talk to us.

(Professor): Hi, everyone. Before starting my talk, I'd like to learn if anyone in this group has heard anything about my profession. Yes, you please.

(Boy): My mother is interested in gem stones, I mean the stones, especially the precious ones that are used in jewelery. She has a collection of diamond jewelery and colored stones. She is a crazed mineral collector as well. She has specimens from all over the world, much of it self-collected. Because whenever she goes to an exotic place, she finds such places where she can collect stones. Her friend is a gemologist. Once her friend told her that some gem stones are believed to have special powers.

(Professor): Yes, you are right. Let me explain in detail. Gemology is the science that deals with natural and artificial gem stone materials, so we gemologists identify, grade and certify the quality and characteristics of gem stones. Today I want to start with diamonds. Diamonds are formed deep within the earth. Extreme heat and pressure combination under the earth's surface takes a lump of carbon and then transforms it into a diamond. Diamonds are simply carbon. As I said before, diamonds are formed deep underground, but some are found near the surface. The reason for that is that volcanic activity forces diamonds to the surface, so we can say that the places where the majority of diamonds found near the surface are volcanically active places. There may be an extinct volcano or an active volcano that is probable to erupt in a future time in such places. For instance, there might be lots of diamonds close to the surface underground here, because we live in an area that once had active volcanoes. Now let me continue with ………………

Part 6 (Questions 34 - 37)

(Teacher): The solar system is made up of the sun and planets, asteroids, moons, comets and meteoroids that orbit around it. The largest eight objects that orbit the Sun directly are the planets. The other small objects that orbit around the Sun indirectly are the moons, two of which are larger than the smallest planet called "Mercury". The solar system extends from the Sol, which is the scientific name of the Sun that was named by the ancient Romans, and goes past the inner planets and far beyond the heliopause.

The solar system formed around 4.6 billion years ago from a giant, rotating cloud of gas and dust. This is known as "the solar nebula". When the nebula collapsed, it spun fast and flattened into a disk. Most of the material was pulled towards the center forming the Sun and others that are within the disk collided and stuck together forming planets, asteroids, comets and moons.

Let's talk a bit about the inner solar system. There are four planets; Mercury, Venus, Earth and Mars. They are known as terrestrial or earthlike planets. Earth has one natural satellite which is called "the Moon" and Mars has two moons which are called "Deimos and Phobos".

In the outer solar system, the planets are Jupiter, Saturn, Uranus and Neptune. These are accepted to be giant worlds that have thick outer layers made of gas.

Part 7 (Questions 38 - 42)

(Teacher): George Orwell is the pen name of Eric Arthur Blair. He was a prominent English novelist, essayist, journalist and critic. He lived between 1903 and 1950. During his short life, with his writings he made an awareness of social injustice, and he opposed to totalitarianism. He supported democratic socialism.

In his early years, he started to be interested in literature. He was the middle child of three, but there was a gap of five years on either side, and he barely saw his father. His father was a civil servant, he had to live in India during George's childhood. As a result, George grew up as a lonely child. For this and many other reasons, he developed habits that other people would consider weird. He started to make up stories and talked with imaginary persons. This was the starting point of his putting down of every story that he created in his mind on paper.

Orwell is best known for his two novels, "Animal Farm" and "Nineteen Eighty-Four". Both include political issues and have been popular since all those years when they were first published. Both novels have been turned into films as well. "Animal Farm" was an anti-Soviet satire. "Nineteen-Eighty-Four" was his masterpiece. It was a work of outstanding artistry and skill in which he tried to give the readers a glimpse into what would happen if governments controlled citizens' lives.

His other important essays were; "Shooting an Elephant", "Down and Out in Paris and London".

He is still read by millions of people worldwide.

Section 4

ANSWER KEYS

Practice Test - 1

Listening Comprehension		Language Form and Meaning		Reading Comprehension	
1	C	1	A	1	A
2	B	2	C	2	D
3	A	3	D	3	B
4	D	4	B	4	C
5	C	5	B	5	A
6	B	6	A	6	B
7	B	7	B	7	B
8	C	8	D	8	C
9	A	9	A	9	B
10	B	10	C	10	D
11	B	11	C	11	A
12	A	12	A	12	B
13	D	13	C	13	B
14	C	14	A	14	A
15	A	15	B	15	C
16	A	16	C	16	B
17	C	17	A	17	A
18	B	18	B	18	B
19	B	19	D	19	A
20	D	20	B	20	A
21	C	21	A	21	D
22	C	22	C	22	B
23	B	23	A	23	A
24	C	24	B	24	C
25	A	25	B	25	B
26	D	26	C	26	A
27	B	27	D	27	A
28	C	28	B	28	C
29	A	29	D	29	D
30	D	30	A	30	A
31	C	31	D	31	A
32	A	32	A	32	B
33	B	33	C	33	C
34	A	34	B	34	B
35	C	35	A	35	A
36	B	36	C	36	B
37	C	37	B	37	B
38	C	38	D	38	D
39	B	39	B	39	D
40	B	40	A	40	D
41	D	41	C	41	A
42	C	42	A	42	C

Practice Test - 2

Listening Comprehension		Language Form and Meaning		Reading Comprehension	
1	A	1	A	1	A
2	C	2	B	2	C
3	B	3	B	3	D
4	A	4	D	4	B
5	D	5	D	5	C
6	C	6	B	6	D
7	A	7	C	7	B
8	D	8	C	8	C
9	C	9	D	9	A
10	B	10	B	10	B
11	A	11	A	11	C
12	B	12	C	12	A
13	D	13	B	13	D
14	A	14	D	14	A
15	C	15	B	15	D
16	B	16	C	16	B
17	C	17	A	17	A
18	B	18	B	18	D
19	A	19	D	19	A
20	C	20	C	20	B
21	B	21	A	21	C
22	D	22	C	22	C
23	B	23	C	23	A
24	A	24	A	24	C
25	B	25	C	25	A
26	A	26	B	26	C
27	C	27	D	27	B
28	D	28	B	28	C
29	B	29	B	29	B
30	D	30	A	30	A
31	B	31	C	31	C
32	B	32	A	32	B
33	D	33	B	33	A
34	C	34	C	34	D
35	A	35	B	35	B
36	B	36	D	36	A
37	D	37	A	37	B
38	B	38	B	38	C
39	C	39	A	39	B
40	A	40	B	40	C
41	B	41	D	41	D
42	A	42	B	42	C

Practice Test - 3

Listening Comprehension		Language Form and Meaning		Reading Comprehension	
1	B	1	B	1	C
2	D	2	C	2	D
3	C	3	A	3	B
4	A	4	B	4	A
5	D	5	C	5	D
6	B	6	C	6	A
7	C	7	B	7	C
8	B	8	C	8	D
9	D	9	A	9	A
10	C	10	C	10	C
11	A	11	A	11	A
12	C	12	B	12	B
13	D	13	A	13	A
14	B	14	A	14	C
15	B	15	B	15	B
16	A	16	D	16	B
17	C	17	C	17	A
18	A	18	A	18	D
19	B	19	D	19	A
20	A	20	D	20	B
21	D	21	C	21	D
22	C	22	B	22	B
23	A	23	B	23	A
24	B	24	A	24	B
25	C	25	D	25	A
26	B	26	C	26	D
27	D	27	B	27	B
28	A	28	D	28	A
29	B	29	A	29	A
30	C	30	C	30	C
31	D	31	D	31	A
32	C	32	A	32	B
33	B	33	A	33	C
34	A	34	B	34	A
35	C	35	B	35	B
36	B	36	D	36	A
37	A	37	B	37	D
38	A	38	C	38	C
39	C	39	B	39	D
40	B	40	A	40	B
41	A	41	D	41	A
42	C	42	C	42	C

Sample Answer Sheet

Listening Comprehension

1. Ⓐ Ⓑ Ⓒ Ⓓ
2. Ⓐ Ⓑ Ⓒ Ⓓ
3. Ⓐ Ⓑ Ⓒ Ⓓ
4. Ⓐ Ⓑ Ⓒ Ⓓ
5. Ⓐ Ⓑ Ⓒ Ⓓ
6. Ⓐ Ⓑ Ⓒ Ⓓ
7. Ⓐ Ⓑ Ⓒ Ⓓ
8. Ⓐ Ⓑ Ⓒ Ⓓ
9. Ⓐ Ⓑ Ⓒ Ⓓ
10. Ⓐ Ⓑ Ⓒ Ⓓ
11. Ⓐ Ⓑ Ⓒ Ⓓ
12. Ⓐ Ⓑ Ⓒ Ⓓ
13. Ⓐ Ⓑ Ⓒ Ⓓ
14. Ⓐ Ⓑ Ⓒ Ⓓ
15. Ⓐ Ⓑ Ⓒ Ⓓ
16. Ⓐ Ⓑ Ⓒ Ⓓ
17. Ⓐ Ⓑ Ⓒ Ⓓ
18. Ⓐ Ⓑ Ⓒ Ⓓ
19. Ⓐ Ⓑ Ⓒ Ⓓ
20. Ⓐ Ⓑ Ⓒ Ⓓ
21. Ⓐ Ⓑ Ⓒ Ⓓ
22. Ⓐ Ⓑ Ⓒ Ⓓ
23. Ⓐ Ⓑ Ⓒ Ⓓ
24. Ⓐ Ⓑ Ⓒ Ⓓ
25. Ⓐ Ⓑ Ⓒ Ⓓ
26. Ⓐ Ⓑ Ⓒ Ⓓ
27. Ⓐ Ⓑ Ⓒ Ⓓ
28. Ⓐ Ⓑ Ⓒ Ⓓ
29. Ⓐ Ⓑ Ⓒ Ⓓ
30. Ⓐ Ⓑ Ⓒ Ⓓ
31. Ⓐ Ⓑ Ⓒ Ⓓ
32. Ⓐ Ⓑ Ⓒ Ⓓ
33. Ⓐ Ⓑ Ⓒ Ⓓ
34. Ⓐ Ⓑ Ⓒ Ⓓ
35. Ⓐ Ⓑ Ⓒ Ⓓ
36. Ⓐ Ⓑ Ⓒ Ⓓ
37. Ⓐ Ⓑ Ⓒ Ⓓ
38. Ⓐ Ⓑ Ⓒ Ⓓ
39. Ⓐ Ⓑ Ⓒ Ⓓ
40. Ⓐ Ⓑ Ⓒ Ⓓ
41. Ⓐ Ⓑ Ⓒ Ⓓ
42. Ⓐ Ⓑ Ⓒ Ⓓ

Language Form and Meaning

1. Ⓐ Ⓑ Ⓒ Ⓓ
2. Ⓐ Ⓑ Ⓒ Ⓓ
3. Ⓐ Ⓑ Ⓒ Ⓓ
4. Ⓐ Ⓑ Ⓒ Ⓓ
5. Ⓐ Ⓑ Ⓒ Ⓓ
6. Ⓐ Ⓑ Ⓒ Ⓓ
7. Ⓐ Ⓑ Ⓒ Ⓓ
8. Ⓐ Ⓑ Ⓒ Ⓓ
9. Ⓐ Ⓑ Ⓒ Ⓓ
10. Ⓐ Ⓑ Ⓒ Ⓓ
11. Ⓐ Ⓑ Ⓒ Ⓓ
12. Ⓐ Ⓑ Ⓒ Ⓓ
13. Ⓐ Ⓑ Ⓒ Ⓓ
14. Ⓐ Ⓑ Ⓒ Ⓓ
15. Ⓐ Ⓑ Ⓒ Ⓓ
16. Ⓐ Ⓑ Ⓒ Ⓓ
17. Ⓐ Ⓑ Ⓒ Ⓓ
18. Ⓐ Ⓑ Ⓒ Ⓓ
19. Ⓐ Ⓑ Ⓒ Ⓓ
20. Ⓐ Ⓑ Ⓒ Ⓓ
21. Ⓐ Ⓑ Ⓒ Ⓓ
22. Ⓐ Ⓑ Ⓒ Ⓓ
23. Ⓐ Ⓑ Ⓒ Ⓓ
24. Ⓐ Ⓑ Ⓒ Ⓓ
25. Ⓐ Ⓑ Ⓒ Ⓓ
26. Ⓐ Ⓑ Ⓒ Ⓓ
27. Ⓐ Ⓑ Ⓒ Ⓓ
28. Ⓐ Ⓑ Ⓒ Ⓓ
29. Ⓐ Ⓑ Ⓒ Ⓓ
30. Ⓐ Ⓑ Ⓒ Ⓓ
31. Ⓐ Ⓑ Ⓒ Ⓓ
32. Ⓐ Ⓑ Ⓒ Ⓓ
33. Ⓐ Ⓑ Ⓒ Ⓓ
34. Ⓐ Ⓑ Ⓒ Ⓓ
35. Ⓐ Ⓑ Ⓒ Ⓓ
36. Ⓐ Ⓑ Ⓒ Ⓓ
37. Ⓐ Ⓑ Ⓒ Ⓓ
38. Ⓐ Ⓑ Ⓒ Ⓓ
39. Ⓐ Ⓑ Ⓒ Ⓓ
40. Ⓐ Ⓑ Ⓒ Ⓓ
41. Ⓐ Ⓑ Ⓒ Ⓓ
42. Ⓐ Ⓑ Ⓒ Ⓓ

Reading Comprehension

1. Ⓐ Ⓑ Ⓒ Ⓓ
2. Ⓐ Ⓑ Ⓒ Ⓓ
3. Ⓐ Ⓑ Ⓒ Ⓓ
4. Ⓐ Ⓑ Ⓒ Ⓓ
5. Ⓐ Ⓑ Ⓒ Ⓓ
6. Ⓐ Ⓑ Ⓒ Ⓓ
7. Ⓐ Ⓑ Ⓒ Ⓓ
8. Ⓐ Ⓑ Ⓒ Ⓓ
9. Ⓐ Ⓑ Ⓒ Ⓓ
10. Ⓐ Ⓑ Ⓒ Ⓓ
11. Ⓐ Ⓑ Ⓒ Ⓓ
12. Ⓐ Ⓑ Ⓒ Ⓓ
13. Ⓐ Ⓑ Ⓒ Ⓓ
14. Ⓐ Ⓑ Ⓒ Ⓓ
15. Ⓐ Ⓑ Ⓒ Ⓓ
16. Ⓐ Ⓑ Ⓒ Ⓓ
17. Ⓐ Ⓑ Ⓒ Ⓓ
18. Ⓐ Ⓑ Ⓒ Ⓓ
19. Ⓐ Ⓑ Ⓒ Ⓓ
20. Ⓐ Ⓑ Ⓒ Ⓓ
21. Ⓐ Ⓑ Ⓒ Ⓓ
22. Ⓐ Ⓑ Ⓒ Ⓓ
23. Ⓐ Ⓑ Ⓒ Ⓓ
24. Ⓐ Ⓑ Ⓒ Ⓓ
25. Ⓐ Ⓑ Ⓒ Ⓓ
26. Ⓐ Ⓑ Ⓒ Ⓓ
27. Ⓐ Ⓑ Ⓒ Ⓓ
28. Ⓐ Ⓑ Ⓒ Ⓓ
29. Ⓐ Ⓑ Ⓒ Ⓓ
30. Ⓐ Ⓑ Ⓒ Ⓓ
31. Ⓐ Ⓑ Ⓒ Ⓓ
32. Ⓐ Ⓑ Ⓒ Ⓓ
33. Ⓐ Ⓑ Ⓒ Ⓓ
34. Ⓐ Ⓑ Ⓒ Ⓓ
35. Ⓐ Ⓑ Ⓒ Ⓓ
36. Ⓐ Ⓑ Ⓒ Ⓓ
37. Ⓐ Ⓑ Ⓒ Ⓓ
38. Ⓐ Ⓑ Ⓒ Ⓓ
39. Ⓐ Ⓑ Ⓒ Ⓓ
40. Ⓐ Ⓑ Ⓒ Ⓓ
41. Ⓐ Ⓑ Ⓒ Ⓓ
42. Ⓐ Ⓑ Ⓒ Ⓓ

Made in the USA
Las Vegas, NV
21 August 2023

76410277R00081